Physic and physicians: a medical sketch book, exhibiting the public and private life of the most celebrated medical men of former days; with memoirs of eminent living London physicians and surgeons. In two parts

Forbes Winslow 1810-1874. cn

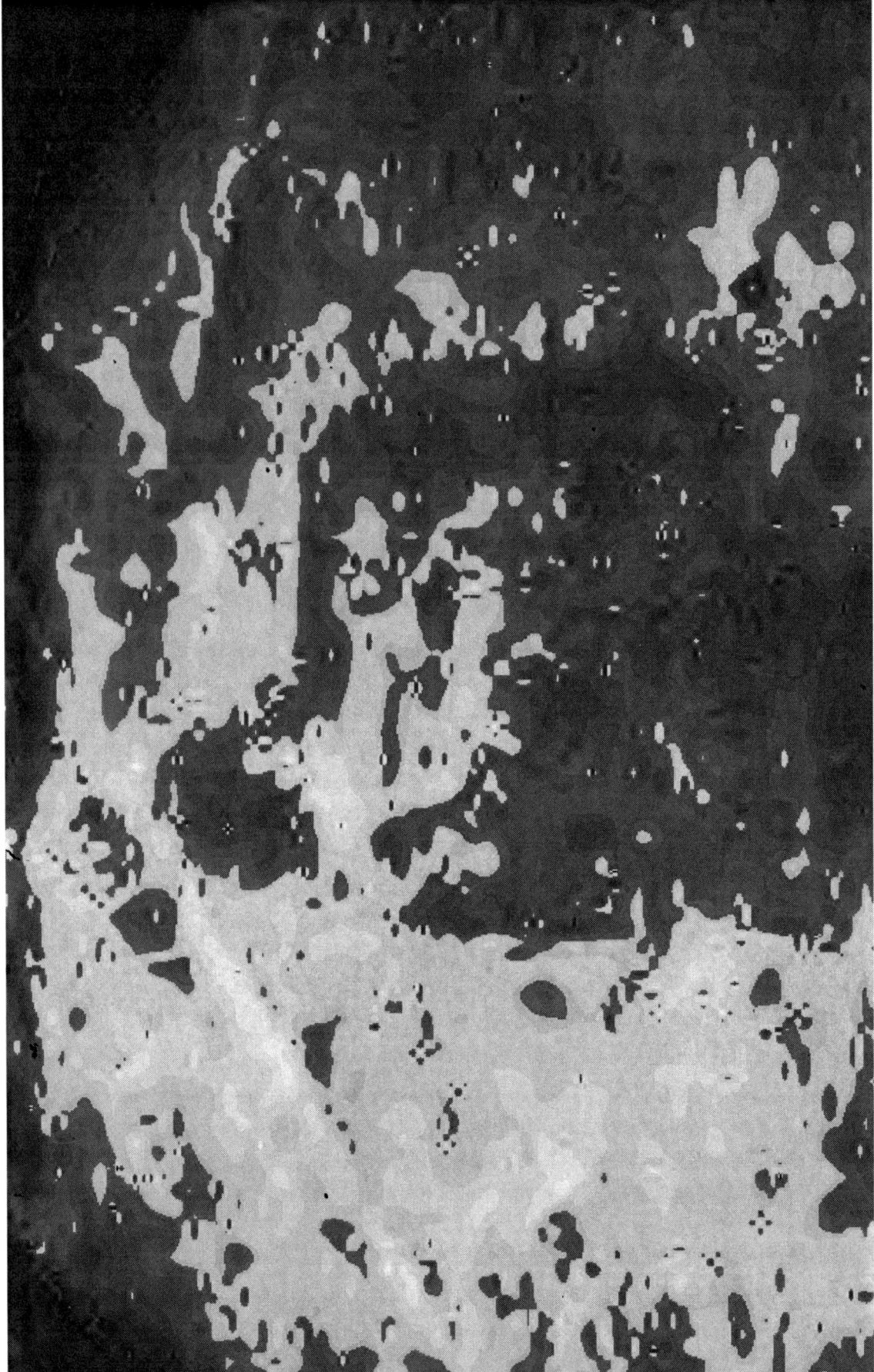

THE HOME & TRAVELLERS LIBRARY

SEMI MONTHLY

XI.

PHYSIC AND PHYSICIANS:

A MEDICAL SKETCH BOOK,

EXHIBITING

THE PUBLIC AND PRIVATE LIFE OF THE MOST CELEBRATED MEDICAL MEN OF FORMER DAYS;

WITH

MEMOIRS OF EMINENT LIVING LONDON PHYSICIANS AND SURGEONS.

IN TWO PARTS.

PART II.

PHILADELPHIA:

G. B. ZIEBER & CO.

1845.

CONTENTS.

CHAPTER IV.

CELEBRATED MEDICAL POETS.

CHAPTER V.

ILLUSTRATIONS AND SKETCHES OF MEDICAL QUACKERY.

CHAPTER VI.

HOW TO GET A PRACTICE; OR, THE ART OF RISING IN PHYSIC.

CHAPTER VII.

CHRONICLES OF WARWICK HALL; OR, MEDICAL AND SURGICAL LUMINARIES OF THE OLDEN TIME.

CHAPTER VIII.

MAD DOCTORS, AND MAD HOUSES.

PART II.

PHYSIC AND PHYSICIANS.

CHAPTER I.

CELEBRATED MEDICAL POETS.

Dr. Erasmus Darwin—Young Keats—Dr. Mark Akenside—
Dr. Walcot—Dr. J. Armstrong—Sir Richard Blackmore—
Haller.

Notwithstanding the discredit into which the poetry
of Doctor ERASMUS DARWIN has fallen, it had once so
great a vogue that the learned poet deserves to figure
among the illustrious innovators of the English Parnassus.
—Darwin, whose poems Coleridge compares to "a palace
of snow," sparkling, but frigid and ephemeral, was ob-
viously the model of Delille, who literally copied some of
his episodes.

The talent of Darwin was rather that of a painter or
sculptor, than the talent of a poet. Accordingly, the
greater part of his comparisons are taken from antique
bas reliefs, cameos, &c. He revives, with grace and
energy, the inanimate form of the mythological divinity,
without stopping to employ whatever the pagan allegory
might contain of dramatic or impassioned materials.

2

Darwin had made himself known among his friends by little private collections of poetry, before the publication of his great work : " With the wisdom of Ulysses," says Miss Seward, " he has bound himself to the mast of science, in order to avoid being seduced by those deceitful syrens, the muses."

The doctor, after having perfected himself at Edin-burgh in medicine, went to practise it at Lichfield, where the good fortune of his first case introduced him to public notice. His marriage with Miss Howard, daughter of a respectable tradesman, was also of advantage to him. His house became the rendezvous of a very agreeable society, of which, the famous James Watt, and Thomas Day, author of " *Sandford and Merton*," composed a part. Miss Seward relates, in her life of Darwin, several amusing anecdotes of the latter (Thomas Day), who was a very original philosopher, and known for his absence of mind. Darwin was one day conversing with a brother botanist, concerning the plant Kalmia, then just imported into our green-houses and gardens. A lady who was present, concluding he had seen it, which in fact he had not, asked the doctor what was the colour of the plant. He replied, " Madam, the Kalmia has precisely the colour of a seraph's wing." So fancifully did he express his want of consciousness respecting the appearance of a flower whose name and rareness were all he knew of the matter.

Dr. Darwin had on one occasion a large company at tea. His servants announced a strange lady and gentle-man. The female was a conspicuous figure, ruddy, cor-pulent, and tall. She held by the arm a little, meek-looking, pale, effeminate man, who, from his close ad-herence to the side of the lady, seemed to consider him-self as under her protection.

" Dr. Darwin," said the lady, " I seek you not as a physician, but as a *belle esprit*. I make this husband of mine,"—and she looked down with a side glance at the animal,—"treat me every summer with a tour through one of the British counties, to explore whatever it contains worthy the attention of ingenious people. On arriving at the several inns in our route, I always search out the man of the vicinity most distinguished for his genius and taste, and introduce myself, that he may direct, as the objects of our examination, whatever is curious in nature, art, or science. Lichfield will be our head-quarters during several days. Come, doctor, whither must we go, what must we investigate to-morrow, and the next day, and the next?—here are my tablets and pencil."

"You arrive, madam," observed Dr. Darwin, gravely, "at a fortunate juncture; to-morrow you will have an opportunity of surveying an annual exhibition perfectly worthy your attention. To-morrow, madam, you will go Tutbury bull-running!"

The satiric laugh with which he stammered out the last word, more keenly pointed this sly, yet broad rebuke to the vanity and arrogance of her speech. Her large features swelled, and her eyes flashed with anger. "I was recommended to a man of genius, and I find him insolent and ill-bred." Then, gathering up her meek and alarmed husband, whom she had loosed when she first spoke, under the shadow of her broad arm and shoulder, she strutted out of the room.

An accidental circumstance brought Dr. Darwin into notice and practice, at Lichfield. A few weeks after his arrival at this place, in the latter end of the year, 1756, the late Mr. Inge, of Thorpe, in Staffordshire, a young gentleman of fortune, family, and consequence, lay sick of a dangerous fever. The justly celebrated Dr. Wilks, of Willenbal, who had many years possessed, in wide extent, the business and confidence of the Lichfield neighbourhood, attended Mr. Inge, and had unsuccessfully combated his disease. At length he pronounced it hopeless; that speedy death must ensue; and took his

leave. It was *then* that the fond mother, wild with terror
for the life of an only son, as drowning wretches catch at
twigs, sent to Lichfield for the young and yet inexpe-
rienced physician. By a reverse and entirely novel
course of treatment, Dr. Darwin gave his dying patient
back to existence, to health, and prosperity. The far-
spreading report of this judiciously daring and fortunate
exertion, brought Dr. Darwin into immediate and extensive employment, and soon eclipsed the hopes of an ingenious rival, who resigned the contest; nor, afterwards,
did any other competitor bring his certainly ineffectual
lamp into *that* sphere in which so bright a luminary
shone.

Dr. Darwin married the widow of Colonel Pole. Early
in her widowhood she was rallied in a large company
upon Darwin's passion for her, and was asked what she
would do with her captive philosopher? "He is very
fond of churches, I believe, and if he would go there for
my sake, I shall scarcely follow him. He is too old for
me."—"Nay, madam, what are fifteen years on the right
side!" She replied, with an arch smile, "I have had so
much of that right side!"

After the doctor's marriage to this lady, he removed to
Derby. When Dr. Darwin found his health declining,
he took almost daily excursions into the country; and, in
allusion to that perpetual travelling, a gentleman once
humorously directed a letter, "Dr. Darwin upon the
road."

When Dr. Darwin wrote to Franklin, complimenting
him on having united philosophy to modern science, he
directed his letter merely thus—"Dr. Franklin, America;"
and said, he felt inclined to make a still more flattering
superscription—"Dr. Franklin, the world." His letter
reached the sage, who first disarmed the lightning of its
fatal power, for the answer to it arrived, and was shown
in the Darwinian circles; in which had been questioned
the likelihood of Dr. Franklin ever receiving a letter of

such general superscription, as the whole western empire. Its safe arrival was amongst the triumphs of genius, combined with exertion—" they make the world their country."

Dr. Darwin's great poem, was his " Botanic Garden." It was commenced in the year 1779. The first part contains the " Economy of Vegetation;" the second, the " Loves of the Plants;" each enriched by a number of philosophical notes. The doctor was engaged ten years in writing this poem.

Dr. Darwin's poetic excellence consists in delighting the eye, the taste, and the fancy, by the strength, distinctness, elegance, and perfect originality of his pictures; and in delighting the ear by the rich cadence of his numbers; but the passions are generally asleep, and seldom are the nerves thrilled by his imagery, impressive and beauteous as it is, or by the landscapes, with all their vividness.

The following extracts will convey to the reader some idea of Darwin's poetic excellence. The exordium to the Goddess of Botany commences thus :

" She comes!—the Goddess!—through the whispering air.
Bright as the morn descends her blushing car ;
Each circling wheel, a wreath of flowers entwines,
And gemm'd with flowers the silky harness shines;
  The golden bits with flowery studs are deck'd,
And knots of flowers the crimson reins connect.
And now, on earth the silver axle rings,
And the shell sinks upon its slender springs ;
Light from her airy seat the goddess bounds,
And steps celestial press the pansied grounds."

The goddess thus addresses the nymphs of fire :—

" Nymphs of primeval fire, your vestal train
Hung with gold tresses o'er the vast inane,

Pierc'd with your silver shafts the throne of night,
And charm'd young nature's opening eyes with light,
When love divine, with brooding wings unfurl'd,
Call'd from the rude abyss the living world."

The effects of electricity in paralytic cases are thus exquisitely expressed.

" Palsy's cold hands the fierce concussion own,
And life clings trembling on her tottering throne."

Darwin compares Dr. Franklin, with his preserving rods, to the celebrated Florentine gem, "Cupid snatching the lightning from Jupiter," which the poet considers as a noble allegory, representing divine justice, disarmed by divine love. The poetic scene from the *Gem*, is one of the sweetest little dramas of this poem.

" Thus, when on wanton wing, intrepid love
Snatch'd the rais'd lightning from the arm of Jove,
Quick o'er his knee the trifle bolt he bent,
The cluster'd darts, and forky arrows rent;
Snapp'd with illumin'd hands, each flaming shaft,
His tingling fingers shook, and stamp'd, and laugh'd,
Bright o'er the floor the scattered fragments blazed,
And gods retreating, trembling, as they gazed:
Th' immortal sire, indulgent to his child,
Bow'd his ambrosial locks, and heaven relenting, smil'd."

The following lines are pretty and picturesque :—

" The rush-thatch'd cottage, on the purple moor,
Where ruddy children frolic round the door,
The moss-grown antlers of the aged oak,
The shaggy locks that fringe the colt unbroke,
The bearded goat with nimble eyes that glare
Through the long tissue of his hoary hair,
As with quick foot he climbs some ruin'd wall,
And crops the ivy which prevents its fall,

With rural charms the tranquil mind delight,
And form a picture to the admiring sight."
Temple of Nature.

The following description of the eagle, is a gem :—

" So when with bristling plumes the bird of Jove,
Vindictive leaves the argent fields above,
Borne on broad wings, the guilty world he awes,
And grasps the lightning in his shining claws."
Botanic Garden.

In the early period of Dr. Darwin's career, he formed an intimate friendship with Mr. Edgeworth, who was noted for his mechanical genius. He thus describes his visit to the doctor's house :—" When I arrived at Lichfield, I inquired whether the doctor was at home. I was shown into a room, where I found Mrs. Darwin. I told her my name. She said the doctor expected me, and that he intended to be at home before night. There were books and prints in the room, of which I took occasion to speak. Mrs. Darwin asked me to drink tea, and I perceived that I owed to my literature the pleasure of passing the evening with this most agreeable woman. We walked, and conversed upon various literary subjects. Mrs Darwin seeming surprised that the doctor had not come home, I offered to take my leave, but she told me that I had been expected some days, and that a bed had been prepared for me. When supper was nearly finished, a loud rapping at the door announced the doctor. There was a bustle in the hall, which made Mrs. Darwin get up and go to the door. Upon her exclaiming that they were bringing a dead man into the house, I went to the hall. I saw some persons directed by one, whom I guessed to be Dr Darwin, conveying a man who appeared to be motionless. 'He is not dead,' said the doctor, 'he is only dead drunk. I found him nearly suffocated in a ditch. I had him lifted into my carriage, and brought hither, that we might take care of him for the night.' Candles came, and what was the surprise of the doctor and Mrs. Darwin, to find that the person whom he had saved was Mrs. Darwin's brother ! who, for the first time in his life, as I was assured, had been intoxicated in this manner, and who would, undoubtedly, have perished, had it not been for Dr. Darwin's humanity." Dr. Darwin has been charged, we think unjustly, of empiricism. He had a notion that consumption might be cured by trans-fusing into a person, so affected, blood from the veins of a person in health. On one occasion, when attending a lady who was labouring under delirium, she expressed an earnest wish to take her infant into her arms, and her attendants were fearful lest she should do some violence to the object of her affection, but he desired them to commit it to her without apprehension. They did so, and the result was an immediate abatement of her disorder.

An instance of Darwin's eccentricity is thus related. During his early residence at Lichfield, Mr. Sneyd, then of Bishton, and a few more gentlemen of Staffordshire, prevailed upon the poet to join them in an excursion by water, from Bishton to Nottingham, and on to Newark. They had provided themselves with a good supply of cold provisions and wine. It was midsummer, the day ardent and sultry. The noontide meal had been made, and the glass gone duly round. It was one of those few instances, in which the medical votary of the Naiads transgressed his general and strict sobriety. If not abso-lutely intoxicated, his spirits were in a high degree of vinous exhilaration. On the boat approaching Notting-ham, within the distance of a few fields, he surprised his companions by slipping, without any previous notice, from the boat into the middle of the river, and swimming to the shore. They saw him get upon the bank, and walk over the meadows towards the town. They called to him in vain; he did not once turn his head. Anxious lest he should take a dangerous cold by remaining in his wet clothes, and uncertain whether or not he intended to desert his party, they rowed instantly to the town, and went in search of the river-god. In passing through the market-place, they saw him standing upon a tub, encircled by a crowd of people, and resisting the entreaties of an apothecary of the place, one of his old companions, who was importuning him to go to his house, and accept of other vestments, until his own could be dried. The party, on passing through the crowd, were surprised to hear him speaking without any degree of his usual stammering—

"Have I not told you," said the doctor, "that I had drank a considerable quantity of wine before I committed myself to the river? You know my general sobriety, and, as a professional man, you ought to know that the unusual existence of internal stimulus would, in its effects on the system, counteract the external cold and moisture." Then perceiving his companions near him, he nodded, smiled, waved his hand, and thus, without hesitation, addressed the populace :—

"Ye men of Nottingham, listen to me. You are ingenious and industrious mechanics. By your industry, life's comforts-are procured for yourselves and families. If you lose your health, the power of being industrious will forsake you. *That* you know; but you may not know that to breathe fresh air constantly, is not less necessary to preserve health than sobriety itself. Air becomes unwholesome in a few hours, if the windows be shut. Open those of your sleeping-rooms, whenever you quit them to go to your workshops. Keep the windows of your workshops open whenever the weather is not insupportably cold. I have no interest in giving you this advice. Remember what I, your countryman and physician, tell you. If you would not bring infection and disease upon yourselves, and to your wives and children change the air you breathe; change it many times a day, by opening your windows." So saying, Dr. Darwin stepped from the tub, and returning with his party to the boat, they pursued their voyage.

It is well known that Dr. Darwin had a considerable impediment in his speech. This, however, did not prevent many flashes of keen sarcastic wit. An apothecary, whose knowledge of his profession was, we trust, superior to his politeness, while receiving the doctor's instructions relative to a patient, observed, what a pity it was that a man of his great abilities should stammer so much. "Not so much to be regretted as you suppose, sir," sputtered the doctor, "for it gives a man time to think before he speaks."

Dr. Darwin has been called a poetical man of science, a title that will readily be granted to him when we enumerate a few of his plans, by which, like the philosopher Rasselas, he was to control the winds and manage the seasons.

By one plan it was proposed to increase the quantity of electricity in the atmosphere, by way of altering the *climate;* and that there should be a *Board of Weather* established, to determine when rain and sunshine were wanted, and to regulate the quantity accordingly. To aid in this desirable object it was further proposed, to tow the icelands to the tropics; and it was most ingeniously devised, that chimneys should be made in the earth, by which the heat of volcanoes should be turned to account.

Darwin's Zoonomia was characterized as a work of abundant conjecture, and little fact. It was calculated for the speculative man—not for the practical man. The pathology was discussed and dismissed by the judicious part of the profession. It produced no change—John Brown had taken possession of the best part of the ground before, and the extravagant hypotheses advanced in his Botanic Garden contributed to injure the success of his medical system.

The following is Miss Seward's account of Dr. Darwin's death :—

" Sunday, the 18th of April, 1802, deprived Derby and its vicinity, and the encircling counties, of Dr. Darwin,—the lettered world of his genius. During a few preceding years, he had been subject to sudden and alarming disorders of the chest, in which he always applied the lancet instantly and freely; he had frequently risen in the night and bled himself. It was said that he suspected *Angina Pectoris* to be the cause of those sudden paroxysms, and that it would produce sudden death. The conversation which he held with Mrs. Darwin, and her friend, the night before he died, gave colour to the report. In the preceding year he had a very dangerous illness. It originated from a severe cold, caught by obeying the summons of a patient in Derby, after he had himself taken strong medicine. His skill, his courage, his exertion, struggled vehemently with his disease. Repeated and daring use of the lancet at length subdued it; but, in all likelihood weakened his system. He never looked so well after as before his seizure; increased debility of step, and a certain wanness of countenance, awakened those fears for him, which great numbers felt who calculated upon his assistance when the hour of pain and danger might come. It was said, that, during his illness, he reproved the sensibility and tears of Mrs. Darwin, and bid her remember that she was the wife of a philosopher.

" The public papers and magazines recorded, with tolerable accuracy, the nature of his final seizure; the conversation he held in the garden of his new residence, the Priory, with Mrs. Darwin and her female friend; the idea which he communicated to them, that he was not likely to live to see the effects of those improvements he had planned. Mrs. Darwin affectionately combating that idea by observing, that he looked remarkably well that evening; his reply—'that he generally found himself in his best health a few days preceding his attacks'—the spirits and strength with which he arose the next morning at six to write letters—the large draught of cold butter-milk which, according to his usual custom, he had swallowed—excited no suspicions in the mind of his friends.

On the last morning of Dr. Darwin's life he had written one page of a very sprightly letter to Mr. Edgeworth, describing the Priory, and his proposed alterations there, when the fatal signal was given. He rang the bell, and ordered his servant to send Mrs. Darwin to him. She came immediately, with his daughter, Miss Emma Darwin. They saw him shivering and pale. He desired them to send directly to Derby for his surgeon, Mr. Headly. They did so; but all was over before he could arrive.

"It was reported at Lichfield, that, perceiving himself growing rapidly worse, he said to Mrs. Darwin, "My dear, you must bleed me instantly." "Alas! I dare not, lest—" "Emma, will you? There is no time to be lost." "Yes, my dear father, if you will direct me." At that moment he sunk into the chair and expired.

"The body was opened, but it was said the surgeons found no traces of peculiar disease; that the state of the viscera indicated a much more protracted existence; yet thus, in one hour, was extinguished that vital light which, in the preceding hour, had shone in flattering brightness, promising duration: such is often the "cunning flattery of nature:" that light, which through half a century, had diffused its radiance and its warmth so widely; that light in which penury had been cheered, in which science had expanded, to whose orb poetry had brought all her images, before whose influence disease had continually retreated, and death so often turned aside his levelled dart!"

"Young Keats," although he never graduated in medicine, studied the art of healing, and was intended for the profession; therefore we claim him as our own, and place his name in our list of medical poets.

Mr. John Keats was of humble origin. He was born October 29, 1796, at a livery stable kept by his grandfather, in Moorfields. He received his classical education at Mr. Clark's school at Enfield, and was bound apprentice to Mr. Hammond, a surgeon, in Church Lane, Edmonton.

On leaving Mr. Hammond, he entered his name at St. Thomas's Hospital, where he pursued his medical studies. He was a youth of great promise. He became early in life acquainted with Leigh Hunt, who was struck with admiration at the specimens of premature genius laid before him. Hunt showed some of Keats's poetry to Godwin, Hazlitt, and Basil Montague, who were very much struck with its beauty. The following lines, written by Keats on his first looking into Chapman's Homer, were much admired :—

" Much have I travell'd in the realms of gold,
  And many goodly states and kingdoms seen;
  Round many Western Islands I have been,
  Which bards in fealty to Apollo hold:
  Oft of one wide expanse had I been told,
  That deep-crown'd Homer, ruled as his demesne;
  Yet did I never breathe its pure serene,
  Till I heard Chapman speak out loud and bold.
  Then I felt like some watcher of the skies,
  When a new planet swims into his ken,
  Or like stout Cortez, when with eagle eyes
  He star'd at the Pacific—and all his men
  Look'd at each other with a wild surmise,
  Silent upon a peak in Darien."

In 1818 Mr. Keats published his poetic romance entitled "Endymion," which his friend Hunt says, "was a wilderness of sweets: but it was truly a wilderness; a domain of young, luxuriant, uncompromising poetry, where the 'weeds of glorious feature,' hampered the pretty legs accustomed to the lawns and trodden walks, in vogue for the last hundred years; lawns, as Johnson says, 'shaven by the scythe, and levelled with the roller;' walks, which, being public property, have been re-consecrated, like Kensington Gardens, by the beadles of authority, instead of the Pans and Sylvans."*

The following beautiful passage on a sculptured vase, representing a procession with music; upon which the author says, with an intensity of sentiment, at once original in idea, and going home, like an old thought, to the heart :—

" Heard melodies are sweet, but those unheard
Are sweeter ; therefore, ye soft pipes, play on;
Not to the sensual ear, but, more endear'd,
Pipe to the spirit ditties of no tone :
Fair youth, beneath the trees, thou can'st not leave
Thy song, nor ever can those trees be bare :
Bold lover, never, never can'st thou kiss,
Though winning near the goal—yet, do not grieve ;
She cannot fade, though thou hast not thy bliss ;
For ever wilt thou love, and she be fair."

In 1820, Keats published his last and best work, " Lamia, Isabella, and other poems."

Mr. Keats's poetical fancy was of a nature to make its way into notice under any circumstances, and would unquestionably have done so; but the political and other opinions to which his attention had been directed, the public connexions to which he was introduced, and the generous enthusiasm, natural to great talents, which would not allow him to conceal either, soon brought on him a host of critics. This preyed much upon his mind,

* Life of Lord Byron.

and, being naturally of a weak constitution, his death was thereby accelerated.

Mr. Leigh Hunt states, "that Keats had felt that his disease was mortal for two or three years before he died. He had a constitutional tendency to consumption; a close attendance to the death-bed of a beloved brother, when he ought to have been nursing himself in bed, gave him a blow which he felt for months. All this trouble was secretly aggravated by a very tender circumstance, and which nominally subjected one of the warmest hearts and imaginations that ever existed to all the pangs that doubt, succeeded by delight, and delight, succeeded by hopelessness, in this world, could inflict. Seeing him once change countenance, in a manner more alarming than usual, as he stood silently eyeing the country out at the window, I pressed him to let me know how he felt, in order that he might enable me to do what I could for him; upon which he said, 'that his feelings were almost more than he could bear, and that he feared for his senses.' I proposed that we should take a coach and ride about the country together, to vary, if possible, the immediate impression, which was sometimes all that was formidable, and would come to nothing. He acquiesced, and was restored to himself. It was, nevertheless, on the same day, sitting on the bench in Well Walk, at Hampstead, nearest the heath, that he told me, with unaccustomed tears in his eyes, that 'his heart was breaking.' A doubt, however, was upon him at the time, which he afterwards had reason to know was groundless; and during his residence at the last house he occupied before he went abroad, he was at times more than tranquil. At length he was persuaded by his friends to try the milder climate of Italy; and he thought it better for others, as for himself, that he should go. He visited Rome with his intimate and affectionate friend Mr. Severn; and at this place, on the 27th of December, 1820, he died in the arms of his friend."

" Hushed is the lyre—the hand that swept
   The low and pensive wires,
   Robb'd of its cunning, from the task retires.
Yes—it is still—the lyre is still,
   The spirit which its slumbers broke
   Hath passed away, and that weak hand that woke
Its forest melodies, hath lost its skill."*

Mr. Keats's death has been said to have been accelerated by a severe criticism on his poems, which appeared in the " Quarterly Review."   To this circumstance Byron evidently alluded, in the following lines :—

" Who killed John Keats ?
I, says the Quarterly,
So savage and tartarly,
   'Twas one of my feats.

" Who shot the arrow ?
The poet-priest Milman,
(So ready to kill man)
   Or Southey, or Barrow !"

Again in reference to the same notion he says,

"Oh, that the soul, that very fiery particle
   Should let itself be snuffed out by an article."

He suffered so much in his lingering illness, that he used to watch the countenance of the physician for the favourable or fatal sentence, and express his regret when he found it delayed.   Yet no impatience escaped him.   He was manly and gentle to the last, and grateful for all services.   A little before he died, he said he " felt the daises growing over him."   But he made a still more touching remark, respecting his epitaph.   " If any," he

---

* Kirke White.

said, "were put over him, he wished it to consist only of these words :—'Here lies one whose name was writ in water!'" So little did he think of the more than promise he had given; of the fine and lasting things he had added to the stock of poetry. The physicians expressed their astonishment that he had held out so long, the lungs turning out, on inspection, to have been almost obliterated.

"Mr. Keats," says his friend, Mr. L. Hunt, "will be known hereafter in English literature, emphatically, as the *young poet;* and his volumes will be the sure companions, in field and grove, of all those who know what a luxury it is to hasten with a favourite volume against one's heart, out of the strife of common-places, into the haven of solitude and imagination."*

MARK AKENSIDE was the son of a butcher, and was born at Newcastle-upon-Tyne, on the 9th of November, 1721. He is said to have been, in after life, very much ashamed of the comparative lowness of his birth; and it is also reported that he could never regard a lameness, which impeded his walking with facility, otherwise than as an unpleasant memento of a cut on the foot, which he received from the fall of one of his father's cleavers, when about seven years of age. Akenside was always much attached to the place of his birth, as it will be perceived by the following beautiful lines, commemorative of the pleasure he was accustomed to receive, in early life, from wandering among the scenes of his native river :

> "O, ye dales
> Of *Tyne,* and ye most ancient woodlands! where
> Oft, as the giant flood obliquely strides,

---

* The fate of Keats reminds us of what Shelley says,

> "Most men
> Are cradled into poetry by wrong;
> They learn in suffering what they teach in song."

3*

And his banks open, and his lawns extend,
Stops short the pleased traveller to view,
Presiding o'er the scene, some rustic tow'r,
Founded by Norman or by Saxon hands."

Akenside indulged his natural taste for poetry at an early age; for when he was only sixteen he was a contributor to the Gentleman's Magazine, in which he published a poem, after the manner of Spenser, entitled "The Virtuoso." At the age of eighteen he was sent to Edinburgh, with a view of taking orders as a dissenting minister; but he abandoned this idea, and commenced the study of medicine. He made great progress in his medical studies, and became a member of the medical society, where he had an opportunity of exercising his oratorical powers. After leaving Edinburgh he went to Leyden, where he became acquainted with Mr. Dyson, who proved, through Akenside's chequered life, his best and constant friend.

At the university of Leyden, Akenside graduated in physic. His thesis was on the growth of the fœtus. It was during his stay at Leyden that Akenside commenced his great poem, on the "Pleasures of the Imagination," which he offered to Dodsley, when he came to London, for £120. Before it was purchased, Dodsley showed the MS. to Pope, who, on perceiving its merit, told him " to make no niggardly offer, since this was no every-day writer." Dodsley immediately closed with the poet, and Richardson was employed to print it.

Mr. Meyrick, a surgeon and apothecary, was an intimate friend of the poet. He says he frequently called upon him, and recommended Akenside as a physician. " We were not much like each other; for he was stiff and set, and I all life and spirits. He often frowned upon me in a sick room. He could not bear to see any one smile in the presence of an invalid; and, I think, he lost a good deal of business by the solemn sententiousness of his air and manner. I wanted to cheer patients up." Mr. Meyrick was also a friend of Armstrong, of whom he says, "He ruined himself by that foolish performance of his, the 'Economy of Love.' How in the name of heaven could he expect that any woman would let him enter her house again after that? The man was a fool! He who undertakes to be a physician must be chastity itself."*

Akenside and Armstrong published their principal poems in the same year. They appealed to the consent of mankind in opposite directions. For if the poem, the "Pleasures of the Imagination," be rich in materials, and brilliant in imagery and versification, the "Art of Preserving Health" is as remarkable for its simplicity of style, and a total rejection of ornament. Their success, as poets, retarded them as physicians. They associated occasionally; but their characters never assimilated. Akenside was solemn in manner, but engaging and polite; except when unwarrantably put upon, and then he became irritable, though never overbearing. Armstrong relapsed into a morbid sensibility; the languid listlessness of which is said to have damped the vigour of his intellectual efforts to a great degree.

Akenside's poem was published anonymously; but, on account of its being attributed to a man of the name of Rolt, he was induced te put his name to the title-page.

Smollett entertained a great personal enmity to Akenside, who he has ridiculed in "Peregrine Pickle." Akenside intended to establish himself in practice at Northampton, and went there for that purpose, but he found that there was no opening for him in that town. He returned to London, when his friend Mr. Dyson bought him a house at North End, Hampstead; and with a view of introducing the Doctor to the more opulent inhabitants, he frequented with him the long room, and all the clubs and assemblies.

---

* Life of Akenside, p. 30.

Hampstead was not suited to a man like Akenside. The inhabitants were respectable and rich; but many of them not only respectable and rich, but purse-proud and super-cilious. They required to be sought; their wives and daughters expected to be escorted and flattered; and their sons to be treated with an air of obligation. It is no difficult task for an elegant man to flatter beautiful women and celebrated men; but, to be subservient to those who are already vain and supercilious, and who assume in pro-portion as they are flattered and yielded to, is not only beyond the practice, but even beyond the honest patience, of a man enriched by nature, and embellished by educa-tion.*

After residing two years and a half at Hampstead, Akenside returned to London, and took up his abode in Bloomsbury Square, where he continued to live during the remainder of his life. He was then about seven-and-twenty years of age.

"In London," says one of his biographers, "Akenside was well known as a poet; but he had still to make him-self known as a physician; and he would have been ex-posed to many annoyances had it not been for the pecuniary assistance which his kind friend Mr. Dyson rendered him."

---

* Dr. Sewell, author of a tragedy entitled "Sir Walter Raleigh," died at Hampstead, in 1726. His fate is thus alluded to by Campbell the poet:—"He was a physician at Hampstead, with very little practice, and chiefly sub-sisted on the invitations of the neighbouring gentlemen, to whom his amiable character made him acceptable: but, at his death, not a friend or relative came to commit his remains to the dust. He was buried in the meanest manner, under a hollow tree, that was once part of the boundary of the churchyard of Hampstead. No memorial was placed over his remains."—*Specimens of the Poets,* v. 5, 1.

At this time Akenside was admitted, by mandamus, to a doctor's degree at Cambridge; and he became a Fellow of the Royal Society and College of Physicians.

Akenside, shortly after his establishment, became acquainted with Dr. Hardinge, who was physician extraordinary to the king. His nephew, Mr. Nichols, says, "he (Dr. H.) was a man of singular habits and whims, but of infinite humour and wit. He was an admirable scholar; and if he had been uniformly attentive to the duties of his profession, would have acquired the first rank in it. In medical sagacity and learning he had few if any equals. His conversation was coveted by the most accomplished wits and scholars of his age. He was a man of perfect honour, and a more benevolent spirit never breathed. His passion for coursing was one of his most prominent characteristics; but, like all the rest, he made it the source of infinite amusement to his friends. He was a comic tyrant over them all; and I shall never forget an evening of civil war, and another of peace, between these two physicians.

"Dr. Akenside was his guest; and at supper, by a whimsical accident, they fell into a dispute upon the subject of bilious colic. They were both of them absurdly eager. Dr. Hardinge had a contempt for every physician but himself; and he held the poet very cheap in that line. He laughed at him, and said the rudest things to him. The other, who never took a jest in good part, flamed into invective; and Mrs. Hardinge, as clever in a different way as either, could with difficulty keep the peace with either of them. Dr. Akenside ordered his chariot, and swore that he would never come into the house again. The other, who was the kindest-hearted of men, next morning, and in a manner quite his own, made a perfect reconcilement, which terminated in a pacific supper the following night; when, by a powerful stroke of humour, the host convulsed the sides of his guest with laughter, and they were in delightful unison together the whole of the evening. " Do you kn—kn—know, doctor," said he, (for he stammered), " that I have bo—bought a curious pamphlet, this m—morning upon a st—stall, and I'll give you the t—title of it ; an ac—count of a curious dispute between D—Dr. Y., and D—Dr. Z., concerning b—b—bilious c—colic, which brought on a d—duel between two ph—physicians, which t—terminated in the d—death of both."

Shortly after this, Akenside wrote an ode to his humorous opponent.

Mr. Dyson allowed Akenside £300 a year, which was sufficient to provide him with every necessary of life. How affectionately the poet speaks of his kind patron, in his beautiful invocation to the " Pleasures of the Imagination !"

> —————" O, my faithful friend,
> O early chosen, ever found the same,
> And trusted and beloved, once more, the verse
> Long destined, always obvious to thine ear,
> Attend indulgent ; so in latest years,
> When time thine hand with honours shall have cloth'd,
> Sacred to every virtue, may thy mind,
> Amid the calm review of seasons past,
> Fair offices of friendship, or kind peace,   ·
> Or public zeal—may then thy mind, well pleased,
> Recall those happy studies of our prime."

When the situation of physician to the Charter-House became vacant, Akenside started for it, but did not succeed in obtaining the appointment.

In July, 1755, Akenside read the " Gulstonian Lectures," before the College of Physicians. In these discourses he advanced opinions relative to the lymphatic vessels of animals, in decisive opposition to those of Boerhaave. These opinions may be gathered from the following abstract : " That the lymphatics in general have

their origin among the little cavities of the cellular substance of the muscles, among the mucous folliculi of the
tendons, or the membranous receptacles and ducts of the
larger glands:—that their extremities or roots imbibe from
these cavities the moisture, exhaled there, from the ultimate arterial tubes, just as the lacteals, which are the
lymphatics of the mesentery, do on the concave surface of
the intestines; and that the minute imbibing vessels, by
gradually opening into one another, form, at length, a
lymphatic trunk, furnished with valves to prevent the return of its fluid, and tending uniformly from the extremities, and from the viscera, to reconvey to the blood that
lymph, with which they are kept in perpetual moisture;
a circumstance indispensable to life and motion; while,
at the same time, the continual re-absorption of that
moisture, by the lymphatics, is no less necessary to preserve the blood properly fluid, and to prevent the putrefac-
tion which would inevitably follow, if this animal vapour
were suffered to stagnate in the cavities where it is dis-
charged."

Shortly after these opinions were made known, Dr. A.
Monro claimed them, as his own, in a pamphlet which
he published; but Akenside firmly maintained that he
was the original discoverer of these peculiar views.

In the year 1759, Akenside's character seems to have
acquired some stability. He was appointed assistant
physician to St. Thomas's Hospital, and two months after,
principal physician; and in the same year, assistant physician to Christ's Hospital.

Sir John Hawkins relates, in his life of Dr. Johnson,
that a person named Saxby, who held a situation in the
custom-house, and who was of that despicable order,
who have the privilege of saying just what they please,
was in the constant habit of venting his sarcasms against
the medical profession. "One evening," says Sir John,
" after having laboured hard to prove that the profession
of physic was all imposture, he turned suddenly upon

Akenside, and observed, 'Doctor, after all you have said, my opinion of the profession is this: the ancients endeavoured to make it a science, and failed; and the moderns, to make it a trade, and succeeded.' The company laughed at the satire, and Akenside joined in it with good humour."

Sir John Hawkins relates another anecdote, relative to a low-minded man, named Ballow. This person was a lawyer, of great learning, but of no practice; full of spleen: of vulgar manners; and having some connexion with the government, he thought, as many persons standing in the same relative situation would have the ignorance to believe, that he was entitled to hate Akenside for those liberal sentiments which he seldom thought it necessary either to qualify or disguise. A dispute, one evening, was the consequence; and Ballow, having made use of some expressions, little conforming with the manners of a gentleman, Akenside degraded himself so far as to demand an apology, forgetting that beautiful and sublime sentence,

"Affronts are innocent when men are worthless."

Ballow was courageous enough to insult, but not sufficiently so to pay the penalty. He, therefore, screened himself from punishment, by keeping out of the way. Akenside's anger soon subsided; and then some mutual friends adjusted the difference.

Few men ever lived who had a greater inward detestation of tyranny than Akenside. This feeling is indicated in all his poems; and he had an equal contempt for hypocrisy. Considering, with Shaftesbury,* that the Deity was the sovereign source of all beauty, he was indignant when the name of our Saviour was used irreverently. "People would assert," he was accustomed to say, "that

---

* Characteristics.

I imitated Newton, or I should never allude to the Deity, or hear him alluded to by others, but I should make an inclination of my body." And one day, being in company with Mr. Meyrick's father, at a coffee-house, in the neighbourhood of Charing Cross, having listened, for some time, with impatience, to the oratory of a Mr. Warnefield, who was making some severe remarks, not only on "Warburton's Divine Legation of Moses," but on the Bible itself, he at length interrupted him: "I tell you what, sir," said he, "Warburton is no friend of mine;—but I detest hearing a man of learning abused. As to the Bible, believe it or not, just as you please; but let it contain as many absurdities, untruths, and unsound doctrines, as you say it does, there is one passage, at least, that I am sure you, with all the ingenuity and eloquence you possess, have not the power to surpass: it is where the prophet says, 'The children of men are much wiser than the children of light.'"

In 1768, Akenside published three essays in the "Medical Transactions." 1. On Cancers. 2. On the use of Ipecacuanha in Asthmas. 3. On the best mode of treating white swellings of the joints.

In the forty-ninth year of his age he was seized with a putrid sore throat, which terminated in his death on the 23d of June, 1770.

Of Akenside's character, as a poet, let our readers listen to what a kindred genius says of him. Speaking of the "Pleasures of the Imagination," Campbell observes, "In the purely ethical and didactic parts of his subject, he displays a high zeal of classical feeling, and a graceful developement of the philosophy of taste. Though his metaphysics may not be always invulnerable, his general ideas of moral truth are lofty and prepossessing. He is peculiarly eloquent in those passages in which he describes the final causes of our emotions of taste: he is equally skilful in delineating the processes of memory and association; and he gives an animated view of Genius collecting her stores for works of excellence. We seem to pass, in his poem, through a gallery of pictured abstractions, rather than of pictured things. He reminds us of odours which we enjoy, artificially extracted from the flower, instead of inhaling them from its natural blossom."

Akenside's pastorals are superior to any other in the language; and his poem, descriptive of a farmer's life, is, perhaps, second only to Virgil's Georgics.

> " Fret not thyself, thou glittering child of pride,
>   That a poor villager inspires my strain;
> With thee let pageantry and power abide,
>   The gentle muses haunt the sylvan reign;
> Where through wild groves at eve the lonely swain
>   Enraptur'd roams, to gaze on nature's charms,
> They hate the sensual and scorn the vain;
>   The parasite their influence never warms;
> Nor him, whose sordid soul the love of gold alarms."

Mr. Bucke takes a more favourable view of Akenside than Mr. Pettigrew does, in his life of his friend, Dr. Lettsom. Lettsom was a pupil at St. Thomas's Hospital when the poet was the physician of that institution, and having been an ardent admirer of Akenside's great poem, the " Pleasures of the Imagination," he allowed his own fancy to picture some ideal object to his mind, and when he approached the real flesh and blood of the poet, Pettigrew observes, " Great was his disappointment." Dr. Akenside, according to Lettsom's biographer, was the most supercilious and unfeeling physician he (Lettsom) had ever known. If the poor affrighted patients did not return a direct answer to his queries, he would often instantly discharge them from the hospital. He evinced a particular disgust to females, and generally treated them with harshness. It was stated that this moroseness was occasioned by disappointment in love; but hapless must have been that female who was placed under his tyranny.

Lettsom was inexpressibly shocked at an instance of Dr. Akenside's inhumanity, exercised towards a patient in Abraham's ward, to whom he had ordered bark in boluses; who, in consequence of not being able to swallow them, so irritated the poet, that he ordered the sister of the ward to discharge him from the hospital; adding, "he shall not die under my care." As the sister was removing him, in obedience to the doctor, the patient expired.

One leg of Dr. Akenside's was considerably shorter than the other, which was in some measure remedied by the aid of a false heel. He had a pale, strumous countenance, but was always very neat and elegant in his dress. He wore a white wig, and carried a long sword. On one occasion his anger was excited to a very high pitch, by the answer which Mr. Baker, the surgeon, gave to a question the doctor put to him, respecting one of his sons, who was subject to epilepsy, which had somewhat impaired his understanding. "To what study do you propose to place him?" said Akenside to Baker. "I find," replied the surgeon, "I cannot make a surgeon of him, so I have sent him to Edinburgh to study for a physician's degree." Akenside turned round from Baker with impetuosity, and would not speak to him for a considerable time afterwards.*

Doctor John Armstrong, known as the author of "The Art of Preserving Health," was born in Scotland, in the year 1709. He was educated for the medical profession, and distinguished himself at the University of Edinburgh, both in the study of physic and literature. He never obtained any eminence as a physician. He wrote a humorous attack upon the empirics, entitled, "An Essay for abridging the Study of Physic, &c. &c.," which gained him credit as a wit, but was one of the causes, it it said, of his being but little noticed as a physician. He

---

* Pettigrew's Life and Correspondence of Dr. Lettsom. Vol. i. p. 22.

also damaged his medical reputation by his poem, the " Economy of Love," which was full of licentiousness.

Dr. Armstrong, though a man of morbid sensibility of mind, possessed an elevated understanding, and great goodness of heart, and was much beloved and respected by his intimate friends, among whom were Dr. Grainger, Sir John Pringle, and the poet Thomson. It is said that he assisted the author of the " Seasons," in the composition of his " Castle of Indolence ;" the fine stanzas, descriptive of the diseases to which the votaries of indolence finally become martyrs, having been written by Armstrong. The tenth stanza in that poem is said to have contained a description of his character, which is so graphically drawn, that it should not be omitted.

> With him was sometimes joined, in silken walk,
>   (Profoundly silent—for they never spoke,)
> One shyer still, who quite detested talk ;
>   Oft stung by spleen, at once away he broke,
> To grove of pine, and broad o'ershadowing oak,
>   There inly thrilled, he wandered all alone,
> And on himself his pensive fury woke ;
>   He never uttered word, save when first shone
> The glittering star of eve—" Thank heaven the day is
>   done !"

A large portion of his time was spent at Slaughter's Coffee-house, in St. Martin's Lane, where he usually took his meals, and where messages to him were ordinarily directed to be addressed. He died in 1799, leaving, to the surprise of all his friends, about £3000.

His poem on the " Art of Health" is full of charming descriptions and beautiful imagery. It will be a lasting monument of his medical skill and poetical genius. Dr. Wharton observed " There is a classical correctness and closeness of style in this poem, that are truly admirable ;

and the subject is raised and adorned by numberless poetical images."

In Dr. Armstrong's last work, entitled "Medica Essays," he alludes to his having failed to establish himself in practice as a physician. As this work is not easily accessible, we extract the passage to which we refer. "I do not send out these little essays by way of a quack's bill—upon honour I do not: for I have not the least inclination to extend my practice beyond the circle of a few friends and acquaintances; amongst whom I commonly find sufficient employment to secure me from the melancholy languor of idleness, and the remorse that in some minds must naturally haunt a life of dissipation. Though I could neither tell a heap of lies in my own praise wherever I went; nor intrigue with nurses; nor associate, much less assimilate, with the various kinds of pert, insipid, lively, stupid, well-bred, impertinent, good-humoured, malicious, obliging, deceitful, drivelling gossips; nor enter into *juntos* with people I did not like; it will appear a mighty boast to any one but moderately acquainted with this town to say, that I might have done *great things* in physic. Most certainly I could. But my ambition, a great many years ago, received a fatal check from a ticklish state of spirits, that made me afraid of a business, in which I found myself exposed to much anxiety, and a crowd of teasing, uncomfortable, mortifying circumstances; to be encountered at all hours, and in every kind of weather. But for that distempered excess of sensibility, I might have been as much reverenced as any *quack*, notwithstanding I was so imprudent as to publish a system of what every body allows to be sound physic; only, indeed—*it was in verse.* However, it is well that some particular people never reckoned me the worse physician for all that; and as it became the fashion to praise one's self, though I do not say that *none of my patients die*, I have some reason to believe, that in proportion to numbers, whether for skill or good luck, not many physicians have been more successful in the management of dangerous and difficult cases; most probably, indeed, from good luck; and yet I have never been remarkable for it in any thing else. In the mean time I have heard that my character, as a physician, has been ungenerously nibbled at by people of my own profession; which I understand has had its intended effect upon some gentry, who it seems are two shallow in a knowledge of human nature, of mankind, and even of the world, to have observed that people of the same business are *sometimes* not very fond of each other; and that to be an object of detraction, in such cases, is no sign of inferior abilities. However, to comfort and support myself under the dark hints of such illiberal enemies, it is natural for me to recollect, that there are still some gentlemen of the faculty, who have candour and generosity enough among themselves to give me all reasonable credit, even as a physician. But the lies of malice are more listened to, and circulate much faster, than the fair reports of good-nature.

" So much for my history as a physician. As an author too, my fate has been somewhat particular. My having written a poem upon a subject, reckoned of no inconsiderable consequence to the health of mankind was, as some say, sufficient alone, in this age and meridian, to have ruined me as a physician. At the same time, from the treachery of one bookseller after another, it is true enough what one of my friends guessed not long ago—that though my works, as he called them, had sold greatly, I do not believe they have altogether brought me near so much as has often been made by one play that deserved to have been damned."

Doctor Walcot, the far-famed " Peter Pindar," was the son of a medical practitioner. His father practised as a surgeon-apothecary in a small town near Kingsbridge, in Devonshire. Walcot was apprenticed to a Mr. Stephens, of Fowey, who had married his sister. During his apprenticeship, his flute and his muse were of more consequence to him than the pestle and mortar; and his love of amusement and society made him indifferent, if not careless, to the duties of his profession—whilst his quickness and his talent gave him a knowledge of it, which labour and application might have struggled for in vain.

"As my uncle," he says, "was always averse to my shining, I used to steal away to an old ruined tower, situated on a rock close by the sea, where many an early and late hour was devoted to the muses."

When Sir William Trelawny went out as governor of Jamaica, Mr. Walcot accompanied him as his medical attendant. Previously to his leaving his country he obtained from a Scotch university his degree of M.D. He was afterwards persuaded to enter the church, in consequence of his patron having a living in his gift. His talent for satire soon made Jamaica too hot for him, and induced the governor to regret the responsibility he had taken upon himself. He frequently related a story of his own surprise at preaching to a congregation which consisted of a cow, a jackass, an old soldier, and two negroes. "I wondered," said the doctor, "how so many came to hear me, but I looked out and saw it rained." During his residence in the West Indies he had a very narrow escape. He was seized with the dreadful malady of the country, and had given up all hopes of recovery as his attendants had done. His nurse was asleep on her couch. and he was lying in that torpid state which is generally considered a fatal symptom, when he was roused from his lethargy by two negroes, who, *sans ceremonie*, began to place him in a straight position. The doctor inquired, as well as he could do, what they wanted, and how they dare to disturb him? The fellows begged pardon, and with an unmeaning grin, replied, "Only to measure you for your coffin, massa." The doctor was so enraged, that passion literally gave a turn to his disorder. When he recovered he determined, to use his own words, " to play the devil a trick; and if he despatched any more of his emissaries for him, not to be found in the same place." He consequently returned to England with Lady Tre-lawny. After meeting with many disappointments in love, he settled at Truro Green. In this opulent neighbour-hood, the practice of his profession would, in a few years, have secured him an ample fortune, but for his mis-chievous talents, which made persons, however highly they thought of his abilities, reject him from their houses. His muse was never at rest whilst his neighbours could be annoyed. One of the objects of his ridicule was a young man of considerable fortune, and a son of one of the magistrates; he possessed some eccentricities, which the doctor did not fail to make the most of. We quote a few lines from the satire alluded to:—

> " Zounds! 'twould disgrace my very pen,
> To place thee on a rank with men—
> A creature that's by all confessed
> An ourang-outang at the best.
> Observe his dress—was such e'er seen?
> A swine that wallows is more clean:
> Six days at least he's worn his shirt:
> His stockings are bedaubed with dirt:
> A rusty hat serves to contain
> A skull quite destitute of brain.
> Yet some will say—the lad has merit,
> And though he's dirty wants not spirit:
> I know he does his best endeavour
> To make folks think him mighty clever."

One of the members for Truro at that time was a Mr. Rosewarne, a worthy man, benevolent to the poor, but rather pompous in his manner and style of living. Wal-cot satirized the weak parts of his character: and some say that he was the cause of his death.

Mr. Rosewarne was at the head of the corporation, and the son of a man who had kept a little public house in the neighbourhood.

Dr. Walcot called him *King Rosewarne*, and was continually writing satires respecting him. This led to a quarrel with the corporation: and at one of their meetings he thought proper to lampoon them all. The following lines formed part of the satire, and were levelled at Mr. Rosewarne:—

> " Up rose King Rosewarne in a huff,
>   Big as bull beef, as Ajax bluff—
>   Sneezes to clear his idea-pot,
>   And coughs the cobwebs from his throat."
> *   *   *   *   *

A very respectable surgeon of Truro was at that time mayor; and the lines Peter applied to him were attended with rather more serious consequences.

> " A bull-faced fellow with the itch,
>   Came to my house to cure a stitch :"
>   &c., &c., &c.

He was prosecuted for these verses, and had to pay £200 for libel. This circumstance induced him to leave Truro, and bend his steps towards the metropolis.

Dr. Walcot was the means of bringing the celebrated painter, Opie, into notice. He was walking one day through a little village, called Perram, when the rain compelled him to seek shelter in a cottage, whose walls were covered with portraits of an old woman, and the doctor immediately recognised the original in the features of his hostess. He felt a curiosity to know who the *artist* was, for even in these rough sketches there was enough talent displayed to interest him. The good woman informed him it was her son, who was always smearing the walls with a smoked stick; but she assured his honour she intended to have the place whitewashed and cleaned before Christmas. He expressed a desire to see the boy; and desired her to send him the next morning to his house. John Opie, who had never before entered any mansion superior to a fisherman's hut, was struck with astonishment at the fine paintings with which the doctor's house was decorated; and his attention was so entirely occupied by them that he seemed to have no curiosity to know why he had been sent for. Dr. Walcot, however, gave him some materials for drawing, with instructions for their use. He watched and directed his improvement, which was rapid, and the future F.R.A. soon began to caricature the faces of the principal inhabitants of Truro, at five shillings per head.

After this probation, he attempted a large painting; and his first essay was a portrait of his patron, in the character of a druid. It was a very striking likeness, and was exhibited in a gallery at Truro. Walcot was very proud of it, and was in the habit of taking children to view it, that he might judge more faithfully of the correctness of the likeness. In this instance he once more carried the laugh against himself; for one of the youthful cognoscenti, in answer to a question of the doctor respecting the likeness of the portrait, and who it was, replied, "Why, a bear in a blanket, to be sure."

When he arrived in London, Walcot soon made himself notorious, in consequence of his attack upon eminent persons. The king having discovered upon his plate a certain disgusting insect, led to the composition of our author's "Lousiad," in which he ridiculed that event with inimitable drollery. It is said that there was some intention of prosecuting him for this effusion, but the fear of further satire prevented government from resorting to actual proceedings.

" The story of the insect," says Walcot, " is a fact: it was *un pou veritable;* but whether of the garden or body species was never ascertained. I had this from the cooks themselves, with whom I dined several times at Buckingham House and Windsor, immediately after the event took place." It was agitated in the privy council, whether Walcot ought to be prosecuted for his poem ; but —"are you sure of a verdict?" said the Lord Chancellor, Thurlow, "if not, we shall look like a parcel of fools."

Like most men of genius, he fully appreciated his own talents, and was extremely tenacious of his consequence. Being invited by a late Irish earl to dine with him, in Stratford Place, when presented to the countess, she received him with a slight bow of acknowledgment, and at dinner seemed completely to overlook him. The doctor did not like it, neither did the earl. During the dinner the countess remarked that she had never known but one *Irish gentleman*, and that was her brother, Cavendish Bradshaw, who had established his claim to the distinction, by carrying off the deluded Lady Westmeath from the protection of an affectionate husband, and a family of twelve children. Some person present inquired if she recollected that Lord M———t N———s was an Irishman? "Yes, but who ever mistook him for a gentleman?" "His lordship, madam," said the doctor, "I presume, loses his claim to the title, because he has never been able to make your ladyship a *gentlewoman!*"

Walcot was inveterate against the countess; he observed to a friend the next day, "that the man who was married to such a woman, was d———d before he was dead. And if she could peep into a certain place, all the devils would take fright, and leave her the sole possession of it!"

His writings were very productive. Those who condemned his satire purchased his works to laugh at his wit. An old acquaintance once remarked, when the doctor offered him his hand, that he hardly knew how to take it, he felt so angry with him for abusing the king. "Pooh! pooh!" said Peter, "I bear no ill-will to his majesty—God bless him! I believe him to be a very good man, but I must write upon characters that the world are interested in reading about. I would abuse you, but I should get nothing by it."

Walcot always declared that the booksellers had been cheating him publicly for years, and that at last he got the best side of them by stratagem. He had offered to sell the copyright of all his works for a life-annuity. The negotiation took place in the month of November, and the doctor always appointed the evening for the time of meeting the booksellers. He had an habitual cough, and walking out in the evening fog increased it. When he arrived at his place of destination he could never speak until he had taken a full glass of brandy, and then remarked, " that it made little difference what the annuity was, as it would soon be all over with him." They were of the same opinion. The bargain was made, " and," continued Peter, " after I mixed water with my brandy, the spring came on, and I lost my cough." This always pleased him to the end of his very lengthened life; and after he had signed the very last receipt, he observed, " he was sure they had wished him at the devil long ago, and he should have done the same had he been in their place."

It has been said that he was actually pensioned by government to purchase his silence; but it does not appear that any sum was ever paid to him. As to the imputed pension, he himself says, " the fact is this;—application was made to me by the friends of the government, that if I would employ my pen in their favour, they would remunerate me with a pension. My reply was in a jocular strain ' that as for varnishing knaves, I never could consent to it; I had no whitewash for devils; but if they would give me £300 or £400 per annum to be mute, I might accede. This I said without the most distant idea of the proposal being accepted; however, they did accept it: a half-year elapsed when it was intimated to me that something was expected from me in favour of the administration. My reply was, that they had infamously violated their agreement; and that sooner than write for a set of men I despised, it should be void from that moment; and I pronounced it void:' adding, with some acrimony, 'that rascality might think itself happy in passing without notice.'"

Dr. Walcot neither possessed ability, nor attained to eminence as a physician: it was his own observation, "that he disliked the practice of it as an art, and confessed himself entirely ignorant whether the patient was cured by the *vis medicatrix naturæ*, or the administration of a pill." He considered the joints as blocks, the nerves as ropes, and the whole system as a ship full rigged: in fine weather all was lax, loose, and agreeable; in wet, every thing being tight and uncomfortable, disease was superinduced.

One day, when dining with a celebrated bookseller, the host left the room, when some one proposed his health; "No," said Dr. Walcot, rising, and at the same time brandishing a bottle of red port in his hand; "No; let us drink a bumper to our own: for this is author's blood!"

The following is, we suppose, a similar version of the same story. Having called upon a bookseller in Paternoster Row, to inquire after his own works, he was asked to take a glass of wine. Dr. Walcot consented to accept of a little negus, as an innocent morning beverage; when instantly was presented to him a cocoa-nut goblet, with the face of a man carved on it. "Eh! eh!" says the doctor, "what have we here?" "A man's skull," replied the bookseller; "a poet's, for what I know." "Nothing more likely," rejoined the facetious doctor, "for it is universally known that *all* booksellers drink their wine from *our* skulls!"

The celebrated vocalist, Mrs. Billington, was one of his most intimate friends. He was invited one day to take tea with her. Peter was punctual; the tea was served; and to the astonishment of the doctor, the sugar was brought on table in a brown paper bag. "What the devil is all this, Mother Billington?" "Every thing is at the pawnbroker's," was the reply, "and the silver sugar-dish is sent to get the tea!"

The last eight years of his life he passed in very comfortable circumstances in Montgomery's Gardens, Somers Town, and never went out more than twice during that time. Finding his eyes entirely fail him, at the age of eighty-two he submitted to the operation of couching, which was performed by Sir William Adams, vainly hoping that medical skill could repair or restore worn-out nature. He began to think he was wrong when he had suffered the veil to be drawn from one eye. "A rush-light," he said, "was better than no candle."

When the famous Polish general, Kosciusco, arrived in London from his confinement in Russia, weak, and full of wounds, he sent a polite note to the doctor, apologizing for his inability to wait upon him, and requesting the favour of his company in Leicester Square. The doctor, in consequence, paid him a visit. After the ceremony of meeting, the general began thus :—"You will excuse the liberty I have taken in desiring your acquaintance and friendship, as it was from your works only I derived pleasure amidst the gloom of imprisonment. Indeed, your muse enlivened my solitude, and induced a wish to see the poet that had softened my exile, and made me at times forget my misfortunes."

Dr. Walcot died on the 14th of February, 1819.

SIR RICHARD BLACKMORE was physician to King William III. and Queen Anne. He is represented to have been originally a schoolmaster. This circumstance, although not dishonourable to him, was often urged as a kind of reproach. In a satirical poem, published after Blackmore had graduated in physic at Padua, allusion is made to his former occupation :—

" By nature form'd, by want a pedant made,
    Blackmore at first set up the whipping trade;

Next quack commenced; then fierce with pride he swore,
That toothache, gout, and corns, should be no more.
In vain his drugs, as well as birch he tried;
His boys grew blockheads, and his patients died."

Sir Richard Blackmore was the author of a variety of pieces, both in prose and verse: although, perhaps, the generality of his productions are but little read, yet they seem to have had many admirers in his own time; for the third edition of his Prince Arthur, an heroic poem in ten books, was published in folio, in 1696. The following year he also published a poem of the same name, in twelve books. Blackmore appears to have been naturally of a very serious turn, and, therefore, took great offence at the licentious and immoral tendency of many of the productions of his contemporary authors. To pass a censure upon these was the design of his poem, entitled " A Satire upon Wit," which was first published in the year 1700. But this piece was attacked and ridiculed by many different writers, and there seemed to be a kind of con. federacy of the wits against him.

Blackmore lived in Cheapside, and he was termed by his enemies the *Cheapside Knight*, the *City Bard*. Dryden took every opportunity of ridiculing the physician. He said he wrote to the rumbling of his own chariot wheels. Pope also levelled his wit against Blackmore: the following lines are in the " Dunciad :"

" But far o'er all, sonorous Blackmore's strain,
    Walls, steeples, skies, bray back to him again.
    In Tot'nham Fields, the brethren, with amaze,
    Prick all their ears up, and forget to graze,
    'Long Chanc'ry Lane retentive rolls the sound,
    And courts to courts return it round and round;
    Thames wafts it thence to Rufus' roaring hall,
    And Hungerford re-echoes bawl for bawl;
    All hail him victor in both gifts of song,
    Who sings so loudly, and who sings so long !"

Notwithstanding these attempts to injure him, Blackmore flourished as a physician, had a respectable share of
practice, and was highly esteemed by some of the most
learned men of his age.

Mr. Addison pronounces Blackmore's poem on the
Creation, as "one of the most useful and noble productions in our English verse. The reader cannot but be
pleased to find the depths of philosophy, enlivened with
all the charms of poetry, and to see so great strength of
reason, amidst so beautiful a redundancy of the imagination."

In a letter to his friend Mr. William Molyneux, Locke
says, " Sir Richard Blackmore is an extraordinary person.
In his poems there are some exquisite touches. The
most profound speculation of Mr. Newton's philosophy
is thus curiously touched upon in King Arthur, book ix.
p. 243 :—

> " ' The constellations shine at his command,
>   He formed their radiant orbs, and with his hand
>   He weighed and put them off with such a force,
>   As might preserve an everlasting course.' "

" I doubt not," continues Locke, " but Sir Richard, in
these lines, had a regard to the proportionment of the
projective motion of the *vis centripeta* that keeps the
planets in their continued courses." Sir Richard Blackmore was the author of more original poems, of a considerable length, besides a variety of other works, than
can well be conceived could have been composed by one
man, during the longest period of human life. He was a
chaste writer; he struggled in the cause of virtue, even
in those times when vice had the countenance of the
great, and when an almost universal degeneracy prevailed.
He was not afraid to appear the advocate of virtue, in
opposition to the highest authority; and no lustre of
abilities in his opponents could deter him from stripping

vice of those gaudy colours, with which poets of the first eminence had clothed her. Sir Richard had very exalted notions of morality. Upon being asked what he considered was necessary to insure to a medical man success, he answered "that he must, first, have a thorough knowledge of the profession; and, secondly, be a good Christian." It used to be a favourite observation of his, "that no immoral man really succeeded in any department or business of life: he may appear to be doing well, but it is not the case."

Sir Richard died on the 8th of October, 1729, at an advanced age; manifesting in his last illness the same fervent piety which had distinguished him through life.

Among the medical poets we must not forget to mention the celebrated ALBERT HALLER, whose " Poem on the Alps," has placed his name high among the votaries of the German muse. Haller was considered the first who gave sublimity, richness, and harmony to the poetical language of Germany; and twenty-two editions of his poems in the original, with the translations into other languages, sufficiently attest the general applause with which they were received.

Young Haller in very early infancy manifested a remarkable genius and activity of mind. Born of a family which had always been distinguished for piety, he was accustomed, when only four years old, to make short exhortations to the domestics on texts of Scripture, at the usual family prayers. When nine years old he had composed, for his own use, a Chaldaic grammar, a Hebrew and Greek lexicon, and also an historical dictionary, containing more than two thousand articles extracted from those of Moreri and Bayle.

At an early age Haller was placed under the tuition of a preceptor, whose behaviour to his pupil was stern and severe. This rigorous and pedantic education might have nipped Haller's genius in the bud, and would have given another child a disgust to study, but it only inspired Haller with a desire of avenging himself. At the age of ten he wrote a satire against his preceptor, who had been selected for his office on account of his sufferings in the cause of religion. He remained with this tutor until he was thirteen years of age, when his father died. The family was left in narrow circumstances, the tutor was dismissed, and young Haller was sent to a boarding-school. One of his comrades, whose father was a physician at Bienne, invited Haller to accompany him home for the holidays. Here he was surrounded with books of anatomy, and acquired from them that physiological taste, which gave the master-direction to his future pursuits. It was not, however, without some struggle that the love of verse yielded that ascendency ; and on one occasion, upon an alarm of fire being given, the young stranger was seen hurrying out of the house with a load of manuscript poetry, as the most precious thing he had to save. The pieces in this collection were mostly of the same description as the satire on his preceptor ; and it is recorded to his honour that about a year afterwards, when his judgment became more matured, he felt so sensibly how unamiable it was in a boy to exercise his ingenuity in exposing the faults and follies of men, that he voluntarily committed to the flames the whole of that collection which he had shortly before been so anxious to preserve from the fiery element.

On entering on the study of medicine, Haller renounced wine for ever, that he might be certain to avoid the abuse of it ; and in order to guard more infallibly against seduction, he thought himself obliged to observe a rigorous severity in his manners. He began his studies at Leyden, where he found an anatomical theatre, well supplied with subjects, cabinets of natural history, a very extensive library, and every thing that could encourage and invite to study.

There he found himself in company with the illustrious Boerhaave, Albinus, and Ruysch, and took his degree, the thesis for which was on the salivary duct, in which he displayed the knowledge he had acquired in anatomy, and proclaimed himself an observer capable of enriching that science with many important inventions.

In 1727 he visited England, and was introduced to Sir Hans Sloane, who was at that time forming his collection of natural curiosities; and had the pleasure of becoming acquainted with Plumtree, Cheselden, and Douglas, men distinguished throughout Europe for their professional and scientific abilities. From England he went to France, where he was in danger of prosecution for obtaining dead bodies. He then went to Basle, and commenced the study of botany, stimulated by the example of the celebrated Bauhine and Stahalin. It was at this place that he laid the plan of his celebrated work, "*Enumeratio Methodica Stirpium Helvetiæ Indigenarum.*"

In 1730 he returned to his own country. He now became a poet a second time. His poems contained descriptions of nature, not such as the poets have so frequently and uniformly painted—such as were formerly described by Homer, and imitated by his successors—but nature in the dress in which he had himself observed her, when climbing up the rocks, and traversing the eternal ice of the Alps, he had endeavoured to discover her secret operations; poems in which he investigated the depths of the most abstract and difficult questions in mathematics and morals; epistles in which he paints the sweets of friendship and pastoral life; the pleasure attending on simplicity of manners; the soft and tranquil charms of virtue, and the happiness ensuing from the sacrifices which the more strong and austere virtues demand of us. Such are the poems of Haller. The literary world heard with surprise, that the author of these delightful and amiable poems was a physician, who passed his life in the midst of dissections, employed searching out the most secret sources of organization and life. But the charms of poetry were not sufficiently alluring to detach

Haller from the more severe and useful studies. He only cultivated the muses in his solitary walks, in those hours of the night when sleep forsook him, and during those retreats from study which his state of health sometimes forced him to make. At such seasons, his active disposition impelled him to subject those grand, pleasing, and affecting ideas, which arose in his mind, to the laws of metre, and the trammels of rhyme. His immense labours in anatomy, the attentive observations which different diseases require, the necessary and subsequent reflections, together with consultation on a great variety of cases, employed a large share of his time.

In 1736 he made botanical excursions, ascended the mountains of Jura and the Alps, and descended to the marshes of Switzerland. The studies of mineralogy and zoology were equally subject to his comprehension. The republic of Berne established for him an amphitheatre, where he taught anatomy.

Soon afterwards he was invited by George II. to promote the university of Gottingen; and there was established for him an anatomical, botanical, and surgical professorship. This he accepted, accompanied by a young wife, whose personal qualities had captivated his heart, who had borne him children, and who, by the sweetness of manners with which she had adopted his taste and pursuits, formed the happiness of his life. But, this undertaking proved fatal to his dear Mariamne, who died in consequence of an accident which befell her on the journey.

The regency of Hanover gave him every proof of their esteem for his talents; and it was then that he established that fame of Gottingen, so justly to this day celebrated all over the world. He was so truly original in physiology, that he might be fairly said to have been the parent of it. To this end he investigated the study on exact anatomy of man and other animals. Nor was it until thirty years of hard labour, that Haller thought himself justified in publishing his discoveries, which produced an era in anatomy and physiology.

A review of new publications was undertaken by him, in the whole circle of medical science, in natural history, physics, chemistry, metallurgy, and œconomics. He undertook the review of the different articles, besides histories, voyages, and descriptions of climates and soils. By the influence he had with the princes of the empire, he formed the undertaking of Mylius to travel through America.

Haller furnished the supplement of the Encyclopædia with articles on the subject of anatomy, medicine, and physiology. He was offered by George II. the chancellorship of the university of Gottingen, which he refused, as the sovereign council of Berne were desirous of retaining him, and settled a pension on him. Afterwards Lord Marshal Keith, in the name of the King of Prussia, offered him the chancellorship of the university of Halle, vacant by the death of the celebrated Wolf. The King of Sweden sent him the order of the Polar Star:—in fact, all the sovereigns and learned societies vied with each other in evincing their regard for the great physiologist.

Haller's health had been declining for some time; and when he perceived the approach of death, he confided firmly in that God whom he had faithfully served, and prepared himself to render to him an account of a life which had been spent in the study of nature, and in doing good to his fellow-creatures.

Haller desired his friend and physician, M. Rosselet, not to conceal from him his true situation; and this gentleman ventured to tell him, that the autumn of 1777 would probably be the period of his existence. Haller exhibited no signs of fear at the information, continued his usual modes of life, and in his last moments employed himself in marking the decay of his organs. He felt his pulse from time to time: "My friend," said he to M. Rosselet, with great tranquillity, "the artery no longer beats," placing his finger on the pulse; and immediately expired. This melancholy event took place at the age of 69, on the 12th of December, 1777.

Few learned men have been born with so active a disposition, and few have lost so little time as Haller. His life was spent in his library, surrounded by his pupils, by his friends, by his fellow-citizens, his children, and his wife, whom he had inspired with a taste for the sciences, and who all were employed, under his inspection, either in making extracts from books, or obtaining plants and animals. Such was his activity, that once when he had broken his right arm, the surgeon, when visiting him the next morning, was surprised to find him writing, with sufficient facility, with his left hand. In fact, the whole of his life was, in the strictest sense, one continued sacrifice of his pleasure and health to his love of science.

Haller's library consisted of 13,512 volumes, on anatomy, surgery, practice of physic, botany, and natural history; and about 150 manuscripts, mostly written in his own hand. These were offered to a London bookseller, a number of whom agreed to unite in treating for them; but before they had taken any farther measures, the whole were purchased by the Emperor of Germany.

CHAPTER V.

ILLUSTRATIONS AND SKETCHES OF MEDICAL QUACKERY.

An apt illustration—Madame de Sevigné's definition of quackery—The love of the mysterious—A decoction of flint stones—Attested cures—Opinion of Sterne—Mr. Pott—Faith in the physician—The vulnary powder—Anecdotes of the famous mountebank Dr. Bossy—Ignorance and impudence of bonesetters—Mrs. Mapp—Homœopathy—The Parisian quack—Mantaccini—Count Cagliostro—The college prosecution of Brodum—Suggestions for the prevention of quackery.

"If physic be a trade," it is observed (the speculation is put hypothetically), "it is *the* trade of all others, the most exactly cut out for a rogue." There is the absence of all restraint; and the only security for the doctor's ability and fair dealing, is often what is wafted to the public in the gossip-tale of some retainer in his interest.

A transaction which a person had with his watch-maker affords an apt illustration of the principles of charlatanism. His watch having stopped, he took it to a mechanic, in order to ascertain the nature of the defect, and to have it rectified. The watchmaker armed his eyes with a microscope, and, after exhausting his customer's patience, for a considerable time being, as he thought, very sapiently occupied in examining the machinery to discover the disorder, observed that he could do no good to the watch without taking it all to pieces. It was carried to another, who, a good deal to the surprise of the owner, discovered, and honestly told him, that he *had only forgotten to wind it up!*

It is almost miraculous what a little learning can effect in setting off the attractions of that art (quackery), which *Madame de Sevigné* so comprehensively defines in one sentence, as an affair of "*pompeux galamatias, specieux babil, des mots pour des raisons, et des promesses pour des effets.*"

The late Dr. Parr, of Exeter, defined the word, quack, to be applicable to every practitioner, who, by pompous pretences, mean insinuations, and indirect promises, endeavours to obtain that confidence, to which neither education, merit, nor experience entitle him.

There has always existed, in the human mind, an innate love of the mysterious; and mankind have, ever since the creation of the world, delighted in deception, thinking with the poet, that,

" Where ignorance is bliss, 'tis folly to be wise."

A visit to a quack produces a pleasurable excitement. There is something piquant in the disdain for prudence with which we deliver ourselves up to that illegitimate sportsman of human lives, who kills us without a qualification. There is a delicious titillation in a large demand upon our credulity; we like to expect miracles in our own proper person, and we go to the illiterate practitioner of medicine, for the same reasons which induced our poor ancestors to go to wizards.

How true it is that—

" First man creates, and then he fears the elf;
  Thus others cheat him not, but *he himself;*
  He loathes the substance, and he loves the show;
  You'll ne'er convince a fool, himself is so;
  He hates realities, and hugs the cheat,
  And still the only pleasure's the deceit."

Walpole says that acute and sensible people are often the most easily deceived by quacks. A deceit, of which it may be said—"It is impossible for any one to dare it," always succeeds.

If the imposture required ingenuity to detect it, there might be some hope for mankind; but it actually lies concealed in its *very obviousness*. At the same time it must be owned, that, in some cases, no little degree of firmness is required to resist the importunity with which a nostrum is recommended. "I seriously declare," says Sir A. B. Faulkner,* "that I was myself pressed with no little earnestness, by a person not otherwise above par in credulity, trying to persuade me of the infallible powers —of what?—Ye shades of Hippocrates and Æsculapius —what?—actually and seriously, a decoction of flint stones!!! The prescription was grave and methodical. The flints were to be boiled, and the supernatant liquor poured off for use. The lady who advised this precious physic, would do so on the best authority; and not of one, but of many persons of her acquaintance, upon whose word she could place the most implicit reliance."

The charm is in the *mystery*, in all these cases. "*Minus credunt quæ ad suam salutem pertinent, si intelligunt*," says Pliny. Credulity is indigenous in no particular climate. "In Chili," says Zimmerman, "the physicians blow around the beds of their patients, to drive away diseases; and, as the people in that country believe that physic consists wholly in their wind, their doctors would take it very ill of any person who should attempt to make the method of cure more difficult." They think they know enough when they know how to blow; which, translated into common language, means "raising the wind."

Lord Bacon says, "That the impostor frequently triumphs at the bed-side of the sick, when true merit is

* Visit to Paris.

6

affronted and dishonoured; the people have always considered a quack, or an old woman, as the rivals of true
physicians. Hence it is that every physician, who has
not greatness of soul enough not to forget himself, feels
no difficulty in saying with Solomon, ' *If it is with me as
with the madman, why should I wish to appear wiser than
he is?* ' "

> " The world is generally averse
> To all the truths it sees and hears;
> But swallows nonsense and a lie,
> With greediness and gluttony."
>
> BUTLER.

The distinguished features of empiricism are large
promises, stout lies, and affected sanctity.

Addison tells us of a Parisian quack, who had a boy
walking before him, publishing, with a shrill voice, " My
father cures all sorts of distempers." To which the
quack doctor added, in a grave manner, " The child
speaks truly."

The pretended piety of quacks is very effective. All
their bills and books attest a variety of cures, done partly
by their medicine, and partly by the blessing of God.
This is very emphatical and effective, when cant is mis-
taken for true religion. A story is told of a man who,
although he was never ill in his life, was cured of every
disease incident to human nature, and swore to it also.
In fact, his life was a life of continued swearing and
disease.

The late Lord Gardestone, himself a valetudinarian,
took the pains to inquire for those persons who had
actually attested marvellous cures, and found more than
two-thirds of the number died very shortly *after they had
been cured.*

Horace Walpole gives us several amusing instances of
distinguished victims to quackery. " Sir Robert," says

he, " was killed by a lithontriptic medicine; Lord Boling-
broke by a man who pretended to cure him of a cancer
in the face; and Winnington died soon after by the ignorance of a quack, who physicked and bled him to death
in a few days, for a slight rheumatism."

The sentimental Yorick, in speaking of murder, makes
the following observations :—" There is another species
of this crime, which is seldom taken notice of, and yet
can be reduced to no other class—and that is, where the
life of our neighbour is shortened, and often taken away,
as directly as by a weapon, by the empirical sale of nostrums and quack medicines—which ignorance and avarice blend. The loud tongue of ignorance impudently
promises much,—and the ear of the sick is open. And,
as many of these pretenders deal in edge-tools, too many,
I fear, perish with the misapplication of them. So great
are the difficulties of tracing out the hidden causes of the
evils to which this frame of ours is subject,—that the
most candid of the profession have ever allowed and la-
mented how unavoidable they are in the dark. So that
the best medicines, administered with the wisest heads,
shall often do the mischief they are intended to prevent.
These are misfortunes to which we are subject in this
state of darkness ;—but, when men without skill,—without education,—without knowledge, either of the distemper, or even of what they sell—make merchandise of
the miserable—and, from a dishonest principle, trifle with
the pains of the unfortunate, too often with their lives—
and from the mere motive of a dishonest gain,—every
such instance of a person bereft of life by the hand of
ignorance, can be considered in no other light than a
branch of the same root. It is murder in the true sense;
—which, though not cognizable by the laws,—by the
laws of right, to every man's own mind and conscience,
must appear equally black and detestable."

" Within a very short period," says a retailer of medical
gossip, " flourished, in the Isle of Wight, a man who was

formerly mate of a ship. This fellow began his career at Lymington; and, happily for the inhabitants of Cowes, continued it there : I say, happily, for the credulous came to him in droves, and all the lodgings in the town were occupied. He was a blessing to the owners of boats and packets, and the public houses there. This wonderful man pretended to cure the sick, the lame, the halt, and the blind. The applications were so many, that he formed a committee; by whom the patients were to be introduced twelve per diem. It must be confessed that his mode of healing the lame and the palsied was ingenious. He broke their crutches and hung them up in his hall of audience, as trophies of his skill! Some of the patients were cured by being frightened. At length the bubble burst; people were obliged to buy new crutches: others dying, had no necessity for such purchase; and the rest had their excursion for nothing."

People apply to quacks, for two reasons : firstly, because health is offered to them at a cheap rate; and secondly, like drowning men, when honest practitioners give no hope, they catch at every twig. Thus, the love of life on the one hand, and the love of gain on the other, create a tolerable good correspondence between the quack and the public.

" The desire of health and ease," says the illustrious Mr. Pott, " like that of money, seems to put all understandings on a level. The avaricious are duped by every bubble, the lame and unhealthy by every quack. Each party resigns his understanding, swallows greedily, and, for a time, believes implicitly, the most groundless, ill-founded, and delusory promises; and nothing but loss or disappointment ever produces conviction."

That quacks sometimes succeed, when the regular medical men fail, we have no hesitation in admitting. An honest practitioner will not hold out to a patient, sinking under the influence of a mortal malady, delusive hopes of recovery; but the unprincipled charlatan says, " I can cure you—you *shall* be cured—your disease is not mortal, put faith in *me*, and I will put your ailments to flight."

Unless the patient has *faith* in his physician, but little good can be effected. This is often the secret of success. An indigestion, which has defied a Dr. Paris, or a Dr. W. Philip, has vanished before a homœopathic dose, administered by a Quin whose maxim, of taking *as little* physic as possible, is so agreeable to the generality of tastes. It is recorded, that a patient who had been pronounced incurable by the faculty, as a *dernier resort*, surrendered himself into the hands of a quack, whose promises were large and gratifying. The invalid was told that he must not, however, expect any change to take place in his malady, until the expiration of six months. A friend who saw the daily fee, and daily deceit, kindly expostulated with the sick man. "For God's sake!" he exclaimed, "destroy not the hopes which that man holds out to me; upon them I live, without them I die." Thus,

> "From stratagem to stratagem we run,
> And he knows most, who latest is undone."

It is a singular thing in history, that neither thought nor study, nor apprenticeship, nor preparation of any sort, is necessary to accomplish the perfect quack. He springs out at once from obscurity and ignorance; completely consummate. Like Pallas, when she jumped all armed from the brains of Jove, so is the quack. He is cased all over in native brass, from top to toe—armed in scale, like the serpent, and like him, he is not wanting in fangs. Other pursuits require patience, time, reading, and long practice, before the profession is allowed to act. The lawyer studies five years, the surgeon, the physician, the apothecary, the painter, and the sculptor, as many: the shoemaker, the carpenter, the joiner, each has his long period of probation. But the quack has *none!* He is utterly ignorant of simples. The natures of the com-

monest herbs are unknown to him.   He is ignorant of the
alphabet of medicine.   *Yet he thrives.*   He runs laughing
through (*and at*) the world.

"Ridet, Æternumque ridebit."

A celebrated quack was once visited by an old acquaintance, from the country. (They had been parish
boys together, had tossed dumps into a hole together, and
had cheated each other at marbles.) "*I'm glad to see
thee'st got on so vinely Zam,*" said the rustic; "*but how
is't, man?   Thee know'st thee never had no more brains
nor a pumpkin.*" He was proceeding in this agreeable
manner when the quack took him to the window, and
bade him count the passers by.   After the lapse of a
minute or two, he inquired how many had passed: the
tiller of land answered, "*nointy*—or mayhap, a *hundred.*"
"And how many wise men do you suppose were amongst
this hundred?" said the other.   "Mayhap, ONE," was the
reply.   "Well," returned the quack, "*all the rest are
mine.*"
The story is, perhaps, somewhat musty, but it is a good
story nevertheless, and comprehends a moral.   When we
disclaim against the iniquity of quacks, we should at the
same time laugh to death the folly of those who seek them.
They are the cause of quackery.   *They* are as much
answerable for the spreading of the vice, as the mother is,
who feeds her favourite fool with stolen sweets, and wails
over his misdeeds at the gallows.   If the gaping block-
head, and vapouring coxcomb, did not loiter and swagger
about the streets of London, with pockets crying to be
picked, the picker would turn his hand to an useful trade.
He would never require either the pump or the tread-mill.
The followers of quacks are the cause of quackery.   They
are the cause of all the atrocious homicides that have
ever been committed.   One simpleton bears testimony to
Mr. Quackall's virtues; another to his manners; a third·

attests his wonderful cures. Nothing was ever so sudden, so certain, or so marvellous! His 'vonderful vonders,' as Mathews justly called them, are the theme of the tea-table, and the gossip of the nursery.

The witnesses are not to be withstood. One blows his penny-trumpet, another winds his horn, a third cackles, a fourth brays, and the end is—what? Why, that another victim is added to the list, and the fame of the brute-deity extended! The proselytes of an idiot of this sort are its basest flatterers; but it must be owned, they are also efficient friends. They stick at nothing for his sake. Having themselves taken his merits upon trust, they insist upon propagating them after the same fashion. They assure their friends that "*The universal antimorbous drops*," have cured twenty thousand people in one year, all of them given over by regular physicians. They are sceptics of the faculty; but idolaters of any empiric. They would faint with shame, were they forced to walk from Temple-Bar to Tyburn, with fools' caps on their heads; yet they swallow the most monstrous absurdities, without fear or shame. They are the jest of their companions, and the contempt of all the world besides; but for the sake of some brazen apostle, they submit and humble themselves to the dust. "Ay, tread on me! spit on me! despise me!" are the words of the illustrious Mawworm; "I likes it!" and so say they. "*They likes it!*" Nevertheless, such likings or dislikings, is not the only things to be heeded. It is no answer to the mother-less child (who asks, "*Where is my mother?*") to say "we delivered her over to old Martin Van Butchell! We considered that he, having painted his pony, was fully qualified to doctor her; but, poor woman!—she died somehow, under his infallible method."*

An empiric says, to a person with a complaint in the

---

* See an excellent article in Fraser's Magazine on Empiricism.

organ of hearing, "Sir, you must apply blisters; I know from experience they will remove affections of the ears." If a second consults him, the same remedy is proposed; the same to the third, a fourth, and—for in fact he possesses but one remedy for all the varieties of the disease of this organ, though arising from the most opposite causes; in one, perhaps from some mechanical obstruction, as from hardened wax, and plugging up of the meatus; in another, from an inflammation of the membrane lining the ears; and in a fourth, from some affection of the portio mollis, or branch of the auditory nerve, that is spread over the windings of the cochlea.

"The great evil of quackery and secret remedies," says Sir G. Blane, "is the false confidence which is inspired to the exclusion of other and better remedies."*

A person labouring under an affection of the heart or lungs, is induced by some puffing advertisement to try the wonderful efficacy of a particular pill. He does so, and finds himself no better: "Persevere," says Mr. Morison, "you cannot expect any good to result until the 'Universal' has had a fair trial." The patient acts upon the quack's advice, and swallows the pills by thirties and fifties at a time, until he finds himself advancing, as the Irishman said, backwards; and it is not until the disease has obtained a firm grasp of his constitution, that he discovers he has been trifling with his very existence. Application is then made to the physician and surgeon; and a degree of astonishment is expressed when the patient is told that his disease is of a serious, perhaps, fatal character. Who has he to blame but himself? He placed his life in the hands of a man ignorant of the first elements of medicine, and swallows his nostrums, and then wonders at the result!

A knowledge of medicine is supposed by those who patronise quacks, to come by intuition. The boy who

---

* Medical Logic.

carries his master's medicine to the patients, no sooner is emancipated from the shop, than he commences business on his own account, thinking, like the parish clerk, who announced his intention to go into orders, that "*it is the duty of every one to rise to the top in his profession!*"

The vulnary powder, and tincture of the Sulphur of Venus are said to have performed wonders, one of which Dr. Colebatch relates of a Mr. Pool, "who was run through the body with a sword, and lost four quarts of blood. The medicine being applied, the bleeding stopped; on the following day, he was 'gnawing ill-boiled mutton,' and drank a quart of ale: and in the course of five days he returned to duty in the camp. A Mr. Cherry, also, sergeant of grenadiers, at the attack of the Castle of Namur, was wounded in twenty-six places, twenty-three with bullets, and three large cuts on the head with a sword. He lay forty eight-hours, stripped naked upon the beach, without a bit of bread, or a drop of drink, or any thing done to his wounds; yet this man was cured by the vulnary powder and tincture alone, and never had any fever."*

Formerly the mountebank doctor was as constant a visiter of every market-place as the pedler with his pack. Almost all old customs, however, have ceased in our time, and these itinerants are now rarely seen. The travelling doctor, with his zany, I believe, is now no where to be seen in Great Britain; and the mountebank himself is become

---

* Mr. Matthews, the comedian, in his "Humours of a Country Fair," has hardly exaggerated, in describing a quack thus, sending acknowledgments from those cured by his specific: "Sir, I was cut in two in a saw-pit, and cured by one bottle." "Sir, by the bursting of a powder mill, I was blown into ten thousand anatomies. The first bottle of your incomparable collected all the parts together —the second restored life and animation—before a third was finished, I was in my usual state of health."

almost an obsolete character. Dr. Bossy was the last
who exhibited in the metropolis, and his public services
ceased about fifty years ago.

Every Thursday his stage was erected opposite the
north-west colonnade of Covent Garden. The platform was
about six feet from the ground, was covered, open in front,
and was ascended by a broad step-ladder. On one side
was a table, with a medicine chest, and surgical apparatus, displayed on a table with drawers. In the centre
of the stage was an arm chair, in which the patient was
seated: and before the doctor commenced operations he
advanced, taking off his gold-laced cocked-hat, and, bowing right and left, began addressing the populace which
crowded before his booth.

The following dialogue between Dr. Bossy and a
patient, we give verbatim, as it will afford the reader a
characteristic specimen of one of the customs of the last
age: it should be premised that the doctor was a hu-
mourist.

An aged woman was helped up the ladder, and seated
in the chair; she had been deaf nearly blind, and was
also lame; indeed, she might have been said to have been
visited with Mrs. Thrale's *three* warnings, and death
would have walked in at her door, only Dr. Bossy blocked
up the passage.

The doctor asked questions with an audible voice, and
the patient responded—he usually repeating the response,
in his Anglo-German dialect.

Doctor. Dis poora voman vot is—how old vosh you?

Old woman. I be almost eighty, sir; seventy-nine last
lady-day, old style.

Doctor. Ah, tat is an incurable disease.

Patient. O dear, O dear! say not so—incurable! why,
you have restored my sight—I can hear again—and I can
walk without my crutches.

Doctor (smiling). No, no, good romans, old age is vot
is incurable; but, by the blessing of Gote, I vill cure you

of vot is ilshe. Dis poora voman vos lame, and deaf, and almost blind. How many hosipetals have you been in?

Patient. Three, sir; St. Thomas's, St. Bartholomew's, and St. George's.

Doctor. Vot, and you found no reliefs? vot, none—not at alls?

Patient. No, none at all, sir.

Doctor. And how many professioners have attended you?

Patient. Some twenty or thirty, sir.

Doctor. O mine Gote! Three sick hosipetals, and dirty [thirty] doctors! I should vonder vot you have not enough to kill you twenty times. Dis poora vomans has become mine patient. Doctor Bossy gain all patients bronounced ingurables; pote wid de plessing of Brovidence, I shall make short work of it, and set you upon your legs again. Goode peoples, dis poora vomans vos teaf as a toor nails (holding up his watch to her ear, and striking the repeater). Can you hear dat pell?

Patient. Yes, sir.

Doctor. O den be thankful to Gote. Can you valk round this chair? (offering his arm.)

Patient. Yes, sir.

Doctor. Sit down, again, good vomans. Can you see?

Patient. Pretty so so, doctor.

Doctor. Vot can you see, good vomans?

Patient. I can see the baker there (pointing to a mutton-pie man, with his board on his head).

Doctor. And vot else can you, good vomans?

Old woman. The poll-parrot there (pointing to Richardson's Hotel). "Lying old bitch," screamed Richardson's poll-parrot. All the crowd shouted with laughter. Dr. Bossy waited until the laugh had subsided, and looking across the way, significantly shook his head at the parrot, and gravely exclaimed, laying his hand on his bosom, " 'Tis no lie, you silly pird, 'tis all true as is de gospel."

Those who knew Covent Garden half a century ago,

cannot have forgotten the famed Dr. Bossy. And there are those, too, yet living in Covent Garden parish, who also recollect Richardson's gray parrot, second in fame only to Colonel O'Kelly's bird, which excelled all others upon record.

This Covent Garden mock-bird had picked up many familiar phrases, so liberally doled out at each other by the wrangling basket-women, which were often, as on this occasion, so aptly coincidental, that the good folks who attended the market believed pretty poll to be endowed with reason.

The elder Edwin, of comic memory, who resided over the northeast piazza, used to relate many curious stories of this parrot. Among others, that one day, the nail on which her cage was hung in front of the house having suddenly given way, the cage fell upon the pavement from a considerable height. Several persons ran to the spot, expecting to find their old favourite dead, and their fears were confirmed, as the bird lay motionless; when suddenly rising, she exclaimed, " Broke my head, by ——!'" Every one believed it to be so, when suddenly she climbed up with her beak and claw, and burst into a loud fit of laughter.

Every village, town, and hamlet in the country has its bone-setter. Country surgeons are supposed to be ignorant of the art of setting fractures and reducing dislocations. Why it should be so, it is difficult to say. A person meets with an accident, and applies to his surgeon for advice under the notion that some "little bone" is broken, or out of its proper situation. The surgeon, after examining the nature of the injury, declares that it is only a simple contusion or sprain, and recommends some external application to the part. The patient does not find immediate relief, and being unable to walk, or use the injured part, he applies to the "bone-setter," who, after well scrutinizing the disabled limb, declares that a little bone is broken, and expresses his astonishment that the patient did not apply to him before.

We were once called in to attend a man in the country, who had been thrown from his horse and had injured his ankle. Upon examination it was discovered that no bone had been displaced or fractured, it was simply a severe bruise. There being considerable inflammation, leeches were applied, in conjunction with fomentations. The patient in a few days was considerably relieved, but still unable to put his foot to the ground. This inability continuing a few days longer, the patient and his friends got alarmed, and the foolish man was persuaded to send for the " bone-setter." We called to see the patient one afternoon, when to our surprise, we found our rival busily engaged in strapping the patient's leg. The patient cried, " Doctor, there was a bone broken in the ankle which you did not detect." " There was no such thing," we replied. " Yes," said the bone-setter, " there was, and I have now put it all right." We said, with considerable indignation, " It is a falsehood; and we defy you to describe the position, or even to tell the *name* of the bone which you declare to be broken." The bone-setter evidently appeared confused, but suddenly resuming his *non chalance*, replied: " Oh, that is a pretty question—that is my business—I am not compelled to instruct you in the secrets of my profession. If I tell you, you will be as wise as myself." The patient and his friends appeared perfectly satisfied with the quack's ready reply. Whatever may be the nature of the injury, the bone-setter is sure to declare that a bone is dislocated or fractured, and how are the poor dupes who apply for such advice to detect his ignorance ?

Bone-setting is regarded by the country people as totally unconnected with surgical science, and as an affair on a level with farriery; as easily acquired, and, like a heritage, capable of being transmitted from father to son.

All of us remember to have heard of the celebrated Mrs. Mapp, the bone-setter of Epsom. She was the daughter of a man named Wallis, a quack at Hindon, in Wiltshire, and sister to the celebrated " Polly Peachum," who married the Duke of Bolton. Upon some family quarrel, Sally Wallis left her professional parent, and wandered up and down the country in a miserable condition, calling herself " Crazy Sally," and pursuing in her perambulations a course which fairly justified the title.

Arriving at last at Epsom, she succeeded in humbugging the worthy bumpkins of that place, so decidedly, that a subscription was set on foot to keep her among them; but her fame extending to the metropolis, the dupes of London, a numerous class then as well as now, thought it no trouble to go ten miles to see the conjuror, till at length, she was pleased to bless the afflicted London with her presence, and once a week drove to the Grecian Coffee-House in a coach and six with out-riders! It was in one of these journeys, passing through Kent Street, in the Borough, that being taken for a certain woman of quality from the Electorate in Germany, a great mob followed, and bestowed on her many bitter reproaches, till madam, perceiving some mistake, looked out of the window, and accosted them in this gentle manner: " D—— your bloods, don't you know me? I am Mrs. Mapp, the *bone-setter!*" upon which announcement the crowd rent the air with loud huzzas.

That she was likely to express herself in these terms, seems very natural from her origin and history; but that she should be on visiting-terms with decent people, and associate with persons of quality, is indeed extraordinary. Mr. Pott, who wrote with the pen of a master, has noticed this in no very gracious terms: " We all remember," says he, " that even the absurdities and impracticability of her own promises and engagements, were by no means equal to the expectations and credulity of those who ran after her; that is, of all ranks and degrees of people, from the lowest labourer or mechanic, up to those of the most exalted rank and station; several of whom not only did not hesitate to believe implicitly the most extravagant assertions of an ignorant, illiberal, drunken, female savage; but even solicited her company—at least, seemed to enjoy her society."

Mrs. Mapp succeeded those great quacks, Taylor and Ward, as related by the Grubb Street laureate of the day, who sung :—

> " In physic as well as in fashion we find,
> The newest has always the run of mankind.
> Forgot is the bustle, 'bout Taylor and Ward;
> Now Mapp's all the cry, and her fame's on record.
> So what signifies learning or going to school,
> When a woman can do without reason or rule."

Every age has its peculiar delusion. It was Voltaire who said, alluding to the election for members of parliament, " that Englishmen went mad every seven years." Had he lived in the present day, and witnessed the infatuation exhibited for every startling medical humbug, he would have felt disposed to think that a certain portion of the nation had annual fits of mental derangement. No sooner does one species of quackery bud into existence, flourish, and retire to the tomb of all the Capulets, than another starts into life and activity, exciting the admiration of all the old women and weak-minded men, ever ready to swallow the most incredulous and preposterous stories as if they were delighted in being imposed upon.

The most striking delusion or monomania of the present day, is that of the *homœopathists*—the infinitesimal doctors who believe in the virtues of the *millionth*, *billionth*, and *trillionth* part of a grain of magnesia and rhubarb, and predict the most wonderful cures to result from the exhibition of these unappreciable doses of medicine.

DOCTOR QUIN, we understand, is amassing considerable wealth by his homœopathic practice; and yet, when ill himself, he places no faith in his own doctrine, but sends for his allopathic friend, Mr. Liston. This is one of the grossest delusions ever practised on the credulity of the public, and which men of honour and principle ought to shrink from, as one would do from the sting of an adder.

The principle upon which the system is founded is, to a certain extent, true, and we quarrel not with it; but we do with its general application. How easy it is for an unprincipled man, professing to practice the homœopathic doctrine, to deceive his patients, and to cure them on allopathic principles, leading them all the time to believe that he is doing the reverse. Who can tell that the powders which these quacks give, contain such minute doses of medicine? We have only their word for it, and are they to be trusted? An allopathic physician, when requested to prescribe for a patient, writes a prescription which any chemist understands and can prepare. He cannot deceive us; but how different is the conduct of those who profess to practice this new-fangled dogma. It is founded in imposition. Its very essence is deceit, and as such every honest man ought to repudiate it.

We have said more, however, on this subject than we intended. The bubble will soon burst, and then the public will wonder how they could be so easily deceived.

" The homœopathic system, sir, just suits me to a tittle,
It proves of physic, any how, you cannot take too little;
If it be good in all complaints to take a dose so small,
It surely must be better still to take *no dose at all.*"

This is sound logic and we recommend our homœopathic readers to lose no time in acting upon it.

Some time since a *soi disant* quack doctor sold water

of the pool of Bethesda, which was to cure all complaints, if taken at the time when the angel visited the parent spring, on which occasion the doctor's bottled water manifested, he said, its sympathy with the fount, by being thrown into a state of perturbation. Hundreds of fools were induced to purchase the Bethesda-water, and watched for the commotion and the consequence, with the result to be expected. At last one, less patient than the rest, went to the quack, and complained that though he had kept his eye constantly on the water for a whole year, he had never yet discovered any thing like the signs of an angel in his bottle.

"That's extremely strange," exclaimed the doctor, " what sized bottle did you buy, sir?"

Patient. A half-guinea one, doctor."

Doctor. Oh, that accounts for it. The half-guinea bottles contain so small a quantity of the invaluable Bethesda-water, that the agitation is scarcely perceptible; but if you buy a five-guinea bottle, and watch it well, you will in due time, see the commotion quite plainly, sympathizing with that of the pool when visited by the angel.

The patient bought the five-guinea bottle as advised, and kept a sharp look-out for the angel until the day of his death.

One of the most impudent quacks ever known, was MONSIEUR VILLARS, of Paris, who lived about 1728. When a funeral passed, he would shrug up his shoulders in pity, saying, " If the deceased had taken his medicine, he would not be where he is." At length his nostrum got into fame, and the quack amassed wealth. His prescription with his medicine (which was nothing more than the water of the Seine, and a little nitre), or rather his observation, was generally this:—" It is your own fault if you be not perfectly cured; you have been intemperate, and incontinent; renounce these vices, and with the aid of my medicine, you will live to a good old age." The Abbé Pous extolled this quack, and gave him the preference to Mareschal de Villars. "The latter (said he) kills men; the former prolongs their existence."

Sir William Read, a quack doctor, died in 1715. He was knighted by Queen Anne, on which occasion the following lines were written on him by Mr. Gevonnett:—

> "The Queen, like Heaven, shines equally on all,
> Her favours now without distinction fall;
> Great Read, and slender Hannes, both knighted, show
> That none their honours shall to merit owe;
> That Popish doctrine is exploded quite,
> Or Ralph had been no duke, and Read no knight;
> That none may *virtue* or their learning plead,
> This has no *grace*, and that can hardly *read*."

A quack, who lived in the time of Louis XI., told the king, that a lady whom his majesty delighted to honour, would die in eight days, which having happened, the king caused the quack to be brought before him, and commanded his servants not to fail to throw him out of the window, when he gave a specified signal. As soon as the king saw him, he observed, "You pretend to understand astrology as well as medicine, and to know so exactly the fate of others, tell me, this moment, what will be yours, and how long you have to live?" "Sire," answered he, without exhibiting any symptoms of fear, "I shall die just three days before your majesty." The ready answer of the quack saved his life.

The Duke de Rohan being taken ill in Switzerland, sent for one of the most famous physicians, who called himself Monsieur Thiband. "Your face, Sir," said the duke to him, "is not quite unknown to me, I think. Pray where have I seen you before?" "At Paris, perhaps, my lord duke, when I had the honour to be farrier to your grace's stables. I have now a great reputation as a physician. I treat the Swiss as I used to do your horses, and I find, in general, I succeed as well. I must request your grace not to make me known, for if so, I shall be ruined."

In the memoirs of Mrs. Thomas, known in the literary world by the poetical name of Corinna, is the following story, which shows such a degree of extravagant credulity, as almost to surpass belief, were it not that we are assured that Sir Richard Steel was a sufferer by the same imposition, and that even the philosophic Boyle allowed himself to be deceived. The mother of Mrs. Thomas became acquainted with a person who was denominated a conjuror, and capable of raising the devil. Mrs. Thomas discerning in this man a genius which might be turned to better purposes than deceiving the country people, desired him not to hide his talent, but to push himself on in the world by the abilities of which he seemed possessed. "Madam," said he, "I am now to fiddle to asses; but I am finishing a great work, which will make those asses fiddle to me." She then asked what that work might be? He replied, "his life was at stake if it were known, but he found her a lady of such uncommon candour and good sense, that he should make no difficulty in committing his life and hope to her keeping."

All women are naturally desirous of being trusted with secrets. This was Mrs. Thomas's failing. The doctor found it out, and made her pay dear for her curiosity. "I have been," continued he, "many years in search of the philosopher's stone, and long master of the smaragdine table of Hermes Trismegistus; the green and red dragons of Raymond Lully have also been obedient to me, and the illustrious sages themselves deign to visit me; yet it is but since I had the honour to be known to you, that I have been so fortunate as to obtain the grand secret of projection. I transmuted some lead I pulled off the window last night, into this bit of gold."

Pleased with the sight of this, and having a natural propensity to the study, the lady snatched it out of the philosopher's hand, and asked why he had not more?

He replied, " it was all the lead he could find." She
then commanded her daughter to bring a parcel of lead
which lay in the closet, and giving it to the alchymist,
desired him to transmute it into gold on the morrow. He
undertook it, and the next day brought her an ingot
weighing three ounces, which, with the utmost solemnity,
he avowed was the same lead that she had given him,
and now transmuted into gold.

She began now to engage him in serious discourse;
and, finding by his replies, that he wanted money to
make more powders, she inquired how much would make
a stock that would maintain itself? He replied, fifty
pounds after nine months would produce a million. She
then begged the ingot of him, which he protested had
been transmuted from lead, and, flushed with the hope of
success, hurried to town to know whether it was real
gold, which proved to be pure beyond the standard.
The lady, now fully convinced of the empiric's declaration, took fifty pounds out of the hands of her banker,
and intrusted him with it. The only difficulty was, how
to carry on the work without suspicion, it being strictly
prohibited at that time. It was, therefore, resolved to
take a little house a few miles from London, where the
alchymist was to erect a laboratory as a professed chemist, and to deal in such medicines as were most vendible,
and by the sale of which the expense of the house was
to be defrayed during the operation. The widow passed
as the house-keeper, and the doctor and his assistant
boarded with her; to which she added this precaution,
that the laboratory, with the two lodging-rooms over it,
in which the doctor and his assistant lay, was a different
wing of the building from that where she and her daughter and maid servant resided, as she knew that some time
must necessarily elapse before any profit could be expected. The doctor, in the mean time, acted the part of
tutor to the widow's daughter, in arithmetic, Latin, and

mathematics, to which studies she discovered the strongest propensity.

All things being properly disposed for the grand operation, the vitriol furnace was set to work, which requiring the most intense heat for several days, set fire to the house; the stairs were consumed in an instant, and as it surprised them all in their first sleep, it was a providential circumstance that no life was lost. This unlucky accident was £300 loss to Mrs. Thomas; yet still the grand project was in a fair way of succeeding in the other wing of the building. But one misfortune is often succeeded by another. The next Sunday evening, while she was reading to her little family, a sudden violent report, like a discharge of cannon, was heard; the house, being made of timber, rocked like a cradle, and the family were all thrown from their chairs on the ground. They looked with amazement on each other, not guessing the cause, when the alchymist commenced stamping and tearing his hair, and raving like a madman, crying out, "Undone, undone, lost and undone for ever!" He ran directly to the laboratory, when unlocking the doors, he found the furnace split, and the precious material scattered like sand among the ashes. Mrs. Thomas's eyes were now sufficiently opened to discover the imposture, and with a serene countenance, told the empiric that accidents would happen, but that means might be fallen upon to repair this disappointment. The doctor observing her so serene, imagined she would grant him more money to complete his scheme; but she soon disappointed his expectations, by ordering him to be gone. Whether deluded by a real hope of finding out the philosopher's stone, or from an innate principle of villany, cannot be determined, but he did not yet cease his pursuit, and still indulged his golden delusion. He now found means to work upon the credulity of an old miser, who, upon the strength of his pretensions, gave him his daughter in marriage, and embarked all his treasure in the same chimerical adventure. In a word, the miser's stock was lost, and the empiric, himself, and his daughter, reduced to want. This unhappy affair broke the miser's heart, who did not survive many weeks the loss of his cash; the doctor put a miserable end to his own life by drinking poison, and left his wife, with two young children, in a state of beggary.

MANTACCINI, the famous charlatan of Paris, was a young man of good family, and having in a few years squandered a large estate, and reduced himself to beggary, he felt that he must exercise his ingenuity or starve. In this state of mind he cast his eyes round the various devices which save from indigence, and are most favoured by fortune. He soon perceived that charlatanism was that on which this blind benefactress lavished her favours with most pleasure, and in the greatest abundance. An adroit and loquacious domestic was the only remaining article of all his former grandeur; he dressed him up in a gold-laced livery, mounted a splendid chariot, and started on the tour under the name, style, and title of " the celebrated Dr. Mantaccini, who cures all diseases with a single touch, or a simple look."

Not finding that he obtained as much practice as his daring genius anticipated, he determined to resort to still higher flights. He left Paris, and modestly announced himself at Lyons as the " celebrated Dr. Mantaccini, who revives the dead at will." To remove all doubt, he declared that in fifteen days he would go to the common churchyard, and restore to life its inhabitants, though buried for ten years. This declaration excited a general rumour and murmur against the doctor, who, not in the lest disconcerted, applied to the magistrate, and requested that he might be put under a guard to prevent his escape, until he should perform his undertaking. The proposition inspired the greatest confidence, and the whole city came to consult the clever empiric, and purchase his *baume de vie.* His consultations were most numerous, and he received large sums of money. At length the famous day approached, and the doctor's valet fearing for his shoulders, began to manifest signs of uneasiness. "You know nothing of mankind," said the quack to his servant, "be quiet." Scarcely had he spoken these words, when the following letter was presented to him from a rich citizen: —"Sir, the great operation which you are going to perform, has broken my rest. I have a wife buried for some time, who was a fury, and I am unhappy enough already without her resurrection. In the name of heaven do not make the experiment. I will give you fifty louis to keep your secret to yourself." In an instant after two dashing beaux arrived, who, with the most earnest supplications, entreated him not to raise their old father, formerly the greatest miser in the city, as, in such an event, they would be reduced to the most deplorable indigence. They offered him a fee of sixty louis, but the doctor shook his head in doubtful compliance. Scarcely had they retired, when a young widow, on the eve of matrimony, threw herself at the feet of the quack, and, with sobs and sighs, implored his mercy. In short, from morn till night, the doctor received letters, visits, presents, fees, to an excess, which absolutely overwhelmed him. The minds of the citizens were differently and violently agitated, some by fear, and others by curiosity, so that the chief magistrate of the city waited upon the doctor, and said, "Sir, I have not the least doubt, from my experience of your rare talents, that you will be able to accomplish the resurrection in our churchyard the day after to-morrow, according to your promise; but I pray you to observe that our city is in the utmost up-roar and confusion; and to consider the dreadful revolution the success of your experiment must produce in ever family; I entreat you, therefore, not to attempt it, but to go away, and thus restore tranquillity to the city. In justice, however, to your rare and divine talents, I shall give you an attestation, in due form, under our seal, that you can *revive* the dead, and that it was our

own fault we were not eye-witnesses of your power."
This certificate was duly signed and delivered, and Dr.
Mantaccini left Lyons for other cities to work new
miracles. In a short time he returned to Paris, loaded
with gold, where he laughed at the popular credulity.

Among our notices of distinguished quacks, we must
not omit to mention the celebrated COUNT CAGLIOSTRO and
his lady. They pretended to a knowledge of a practice,
whereby everlasting youth might be obtained. The roses
were to flourish in unabated beauty upon the cheek of
age, without the aid of cosmetics.

This couple first made their *debût* at St. Petersburgh;
the Countess, who was not more than twenty, used to
speak without the least affection of her eldest son, who
had been for a long time a captain in the Dutch guards.
This phenomenon, of grinding old people young, in so
visible and charming a manner, could not fail to astonish
the ladies, who are generally so expert in diminishing,
instead of adding to their years. They flocked to consult
her; she advised them to use the Count's nostrum.
Treasures followed in: true, the ladies did not grow
young again, but their lovers assured them they did: and
Cagliostro was almost deified.

So well did this worthy couple play this game, that a
great Russian prince became sensible to the charms of the
Countess. The empress heard of it: she summoned the
syren to her presence. The Countess lied so well, and so
audaciously, that it passed for currency, and her absence
was bought by a present of 20,000 roubles! A Russian
mother, whose child was dying, gave 5000 louis d'ors to
recover it: the Count engaged to do so, if he were allowed
to take it home for eight days; the child was returned
healthy and well, but it did not happen to be the same;
he had bought one, after having burnt the original child
that *would* die, to make an experiment of regeneration:
all this he confessed. The money was required back, but
the usual answer, "No money returned," was the result.

They then favoured Warsaw with a visit, and adroitly enlisted on their side the priests and the poor. At this city, and at Paris, these impostors realized large sums of money. Morality and decency forbid us from entering into a minute detail of the abominations which they had recourse to, in order to effect their nefarious purposes.

Dr. SIMON FORMAN, a celebrated physician and astrologer, lived in Lambeth. This man was implicated in the murder of Sir Thomas Overbury, but he died in 1611, before the trial. Forman was notorious long before his connection with Lady Essex, and excited a vast deal of jealousy on the part of the regular medical practitioners of London, by giving unlicensed advice to the sick, as well as by casting nativities; but he was at length able to procure a degree from Cambridge. The following lines refer to him:

" Dr. Forman, in art a poor man,
    You calculate nativities;
And by your almanack out of date, tell a fool his fate
    By celestial privities.

" Though to your great expense, you did commence
    In the famous University;
Yet, by such a hap, an ass may wear a velvet cap,
    And there's the true diversity."

No subject calls more loudly for the interference of the legislature than that of quackery. Yet, the question has so many ridiculous sides, that the public, while they laugh, allow imposition of the most palpable kind to flourish and succeed. It is indeed characteristic of this nation, that the grossest public injuries affecting the state, or the public health, are overlooked, while they afford materials for joke and merriment. When we see one of H. B.'s inimitable sketches, representing the prime minister's neck under the foot of the " member for all Ireland," or the leader of the House of Commons, or the Chancellor of the Exchequer dancing *á-la-Rice*, a long score of indignation is paid off; their obnoxious measures are for the moment forgotten; we are sensible only to present impressions, and feel grateful for the ludicrous association of face and dress. In like manner, when in gazing into a print shop we see the representation of a patient who has been dosed, *usque ad nauseum*, with the " vegetable pills," sprouting out in luxuriant vegetation, as the effect of the medicine taken, to look, " grave, exceeds all power of face ;" and the misery, wretchedness, pain, and death, which we know to have resulted from the use of the nostrum, is forgotten, in the midst of the ridiculous ideas which the print excites in our mind.

Steel has an essay on this subject full of wisdom; but his sense of the ludicrous, both in the pretensions of the quack, and the gullibility of the patient, was too strong to let him write gravely; and he has left us a monument of his exquisite humour, where many perhaps will think it misplaced. He despaired, however, of curing the evil.

It has been suggested that all quacks should be subjected to a government prosecution; but we doubt the policy of the recommendation.

The only instance of the College of Physicians having condescended to notice the practice of a proprietor of a patent medicine, with which we are acquainted, occurred about thirty years ago. Dr. Brodum was summoned to attend a meeting of the censors of the college, to explain his mode of practice. The doctor was punctual to the appointed time, and being acquainted only with the Hebrew and English languages, the president condescended to address him in the latter. The doctor replied, that he did not attend patients at their own homes, that he prescribed only his own medicine, for which he had obtained his Majesty's royal patent, and that, in difficult cases, he always recommended Sir Lucas Pepys, or some other able member of the college. The president observed that he did not wish to interfere with his nostrum, but that they required him to drop the title of Doctor, and put *Mister* Brodum instead of Doctor on his door, and to desist from taking fees. The Doctor replied, that all his fees came in letters from patients residing far beyond the limits of their jurisdiction: but if they thought he was encroaching on their privileges by having his letters of consultation addressed to his house in London, he would request his patients to direct to him at a place beyond their jurisdiction. As to his styling himself Doctor, he ventured to say that he had a right to do so, having a diploma from the Mareschal College of Aberdeen. " I suppose," observed a censor, "a purchased diploma." " I don't know," replied the doctor, " what you mean by a *purchased* diploma; I suppose all physicians, who possess a diploma, paid for it. I should not have had a diploma had I not been considered worthy of it; and, as to my nervous cordial, Dr. Warren, and other learned members of your college, have done me the honour to take it, and recommend it!" To the question, " How long did you reside at Aberdeen?" the Doctor replied, " I have never been there." He obtained his diploma on a certificate signed by Dr. Saunders, who was then one of the ruling members of the College of Physicians! The quack doctor refused to remove his brass plate from his door, and the college declined to carry their threat to remove it, into execution. The Mareschal College, on being apprized of the imposition, came to the resolution of prosecuting Dr. Saunders for a fraud; and, had not his friends exerted themselves, it would have been put in force.

In the " Medical Gazette" for March, 1839, the able editor has entered very fully into this important subject, and has offered some suggestions which it would be well for the public and the profession to take into serious consideration.

Having considered the question in all its ramifications, the writer considers that, to diminish quackery three things are especially required :—

"1st. The improvement of our art. This will lessen the number of those who take nostrums from despair. It is by advancing the art which he practices, that every one must strive to show that his long and expensive education has bestowed upon him a privilege, which the legislature need not guard by penalties—the privilege of discernment.

"2d. The diffusion of knowledge on medical points, with particular reference to the danger of many drugs, and the absurdity of using any at random, by drawing them from the wheel of chance at a patent medicine shop. This will diminish the number of those who fall into the clutches of the charlatan from ignorance and caprice.

"3d. It is necessary to make good advice accessible to every one. Clubs or societies for the insurance of health, must be formed on easy terms; and this will withdraw thousands who now fall a sacrifice through poverty."

With the above observations we fully concur; and if the profession could be persuaded to take the proffered advice, and *act up to it* with spirit, the infamous hydra-headed monster would receive a mortal blow, and both the public and the faculty would be greatly benefited by the result.

CHAPTER VI.

HOW TO GET A PRACTICE; OR, THE ART OF RISING IN PHYSIC.

Must commence with a new theory—Radcliffe's advice to Mead—Never appear ignorant—Old women's puzzling questions—Effect of fees—Tricks of the trade—The magic of a name—Importance of belonging to a religious sect—A talkative wife *sometimes* a blessing—Mystery and medicine—Attention to patients—Value of a carriage—The opera physician—The necessity of being called out of church, and of speaking at medical societies—Mead's advice to a brother doctor.

WE can picture to ourselves the eagerness with which medical aspirants will read this chapter. They have probably had practical experience of what "early struggles" are; they feel no pleasure in dwelling upon the misfortunes of others: the great desideratum with them is to know how to advance themselves in their profession; and their successful establishment in it is the *ne plus ultra* of their ambition. In their estimation the discovery of the philosopher's stone, or the quadrature of the circle, sinks into utter insignificance when placed in comparison with the art of rising in physic.

It has been recommended to a young physician who wishes to get into practice, to start with a new theory. Attempting to prove that the blood does not circulate would ensure a great degree of notice, and prove highly beneficial to him. Were he to endeavour to prove the unwholesomeness of some favourite and common article of diet—the more startling and extraordinary the opinion the better—he would obtain an enviable degree of notoriety. He must be singular and eccentric in his manners; —it is a matter of indifference whether he be brutal, or polished and courtier-like.

"There are two ways, my boy," said Radcliffe to Mead, when the latter was commencing practice, "for a physician to treat his patients—either to bully or cajole them. I have taken the former course, and have done well, as you see; you may, perhaps, take the latter, and, perhaps, do equally as well." Skill in pursuits not very consonant to medical ones, now and then has a great effect in procuring practice; it has occasionally been found to have been of great use to affect fox-hunting, boxing, &c. Singularity fills the general run of mankind with wonder, and from wonder to admiration the transition is obvious.

A physician should never affect ignorance of the cause of a complaint; he should place it in the pancreas, or pineal gland, if he has no other local habitation ready at the moment. He must also be always ready with an answer to every question that a lady puts to him; the chance is, that she will be satisfied with it; he must not care whether there be, or be not, a possible solution of it. A lady once asked her apothecary from what substance castor-oil was made; he (more *au-fait* with the slang of the ring than with the science of botany, a hat or beaver being by the fancy termed a *castor*), unembarrassed, said that it was made from the *beaver!* The lady was satisfied, and, no doubt, considered her medical adviser a quick and sensible gentleman. A patient was one day very anxious to know how long she should be ill: "Madam," replied the physician, "that depends upon the duration of the disease." "I am much obliged to you, doctor, for your information," was the patient's wise answer. Never readily acquiesce in any thing your patient or the nurse should say. Old women are extremely fond of putting puzzling questions to the doctor; and, if he be not able or willing to explain the *modus operandi* of the medicines he may be exhibiting, or the nature of the ailment under which his patient may be labouring, ten to one but that the nurse attempts a solution of the mystery. "My doctor," we recollect hearing an elderly lady observe, "always assents to whatever I say: I think he must be a great fool." A physician should never omit to take his fee, unless he makes a practice of refusing the fees of clergymen: it is astonishing how the *aurum solidum* quickens his faculties. It is the laudable practice of many physicians of the present day to refuse fees when attending medical men. A celebrated Bath physician upon not finding himself better for his own prescriptions, said laughingly to a friend one day: "Come, I think I will give myself a fee; I am sure I shall do better then." The doctor put his hand with great solemnity into his pocket, and passed over a guinea to the other: this had the desired effect. The same physician, on receiving the last fee he took in this world, a few days before his death, said, holding it up with streaming eyes to a friend who was near him, "*Ultimus Romanorum,* my good friend."

A physician of Montpellier was in the habit of employing a very ingenious artifice to bring himself into notice with the public. When he came to a town where he was not known, he pretended to have lost his favourite dog, and ordered the public crier to offer, with beat of drum, a reward of twenty-five louis to whoever should find it. The crier took care to mention all the titles and academic honours of the peripatetic physician, as well as his place of residence. He soon became the talk of the town: "Do you know," says one, "that a famous physician has come here—a very clever fellow, of high academic honours; he must be rich, for he offers twenty-five louis for finding his dog!" *The dog was not found, but patients were.*

A poor physician, with plenty of knowledge and no practice, imparted his troubles to one of his friends.

" Listen to my advice," says the other, " and follow it. The Café de la Régence is in fashion; I play at chess there every day at two o'clock, when the crowd is thickest; come there, too; do not recognise me; say nothing, but seem in a reverie; take your coffee, and always give the waiter the money wrapped up in rose-coloured paper, and leave the rest to me."

The physician followed his advice—he was in daily attendance at the Café, when it was most crowded—sipped his coffee in quietness, and paid as his friend directed him to do. His oddity was soon remarked. The question was frequently asked, who is that grave gentleman?—he always appears absorbed in his own cogitations. His kind friend said to the customers of the coffee-house: " Gentlemen, do not think ill of this man, because he seems an oddity; he is a profound practitioner. I have known him these fifteen years, and I could tell you of some wonderful cures that he has performed; but he thinks of nothing but his books, and never speaks except to his patients, which has prevented me from becoming intimate with him; but if ever I am obliged to keep my bed, he is the doctor for me." The friend followed this course, varying the style of his panegyric from time to time, until all his auditors entertained a high opinion of the doctor's skill; and by this means he soon obtained an extensive practice.*

Once having obtained a " name," the medical practitioner, unless very deficient in a knowledge of his profession, may set the whole world at defiance. The very circumstance of his being engaged in extensive practice,

---

* Coleridge tells a story of a lady who had a husband not over-burdened with brains, but with sense enough to hold his tongue when in company. His taciturnity was noticed, and on the subject being mentioned to the wife, she mysteriously observed: " Dear sir, he is always thinking of Locke and Newton."

will render him more qualified to discharge the duties which devolve upon him—

> " Give ev'n a dunce the employment he desires,
> And he soon finds the talent it requires;
> A business, with an income at its heels,
> Furnishes always oil for its own wheels."
>
> COWPER.

A general practitioner has brought himself into notice and practice, by always riding a pure white horse. In justice, however, we must observe, that he is not the son of Esculapius, whom a certain personage, not to be named to ears polite, recognised on visiting this world—

> " An apothecary, on a white horse, rode by on his avocations,
> Oh, oh, said the devil, there's my old friend Death in the Revelations." *

It has always been found, says an anonymous writer, of great use to a physician to belong to some particular sect in religion. He is sure to obtain the patronage of those who belong to it. The " *thee*" and " *thou*" of Dr. Fothergill, of London, was supposed to be worth £2,000 a year to him at least.†

---

* Porson.

† A Quaker apothecary meeting Dr. Fothergill, thus accosted him : " Friend Fothergill, I intend dining with thee to-day." " I shall be glad to see thee," answered the doctor; " but pray, friend, hast thou not some joke?" " No joke, indeed," rejoined the apothecary, " but a very serious matter. Thou hast attended friend Ephraim these three days, and ordered him no medicine. I cannot at this rate live in my own house, and must live in thine." The doctor took the hint, and prescribed handsomely for the benefit of his friend Ephraim, and his friend Leech the apothecary !

Dr. MEAD was the son of a dissenting minister; and whenever he was called out of his father's church, which was often the case, the preacher would stop in the middle of his discourse, and say, " Dear brethren, let me offer up a prayer for the safe recovery of the poor patient to whom my son is gone to administer relief." It is not said how much this circumstance tended to the celebrity of this once eminent physician, but we have little doubt that it brought him many a patient.

It is a very fortunate circumstance for a physician to have a wife with powers of speech equal to that said to have been possessed by Alexander the Great. If she calls at a house to make a visit of ceremony or friendship, she must enlarge on her husband's numerous engagements, and superior abilities. This species of manœuvring is frequently successful in large watering-places, where invalids resort for change of air and scene. In these places young physicians sometimes affect to be precipitated into redundant practice, and languishing under its fatigues, make themselves appear in conspicuous assemblages, as martyrs to messengers in breathless haste—

" To hurryings to and fro, and signals in distress."

I have known, says the editor of the " Medical Ethics," one of these physicians, who, on returning to an evening party from which *he had been summoned*, called surrounding attention to the golden trophies of his exertions, by holding up to view two sovereigns between his finger and thumb. This ridiculous trick he has several times played, until he has led some to imagine that these identical coins, like the guineas given to the Vicar of Wakefield's daughter, were always to be shown, but never changed.

Although mystery is the essence of quackery, it will be necessary to have recourse to it in order to ingratiate yourself in public estimation. Secrecy is commonly mixed up in medical affairs. It is said that a great city practitioner, half a century ago, had little closets like a pawnbroker's shop, to indulge this feeling of fanciful patients, that they might not be seen by their fellow-sufferers. The Compte de Virey carried this mystery so far, as to make the slightest indisposition a state-secret. He one day called a surgeon to dress a wound in his leg; and when a similar one broke out on the other, he sent for a different surgeon, that the disordered state of the limbs might not be known; a circumstance which was the cause of his death. To a person, who inquired for him after his death, his secretary said: "*He is dead, but he does not wish it to be known.*"

Be careful not to pronounce an opinion on any case, until you have gone through the usual routine of feeling the pulse, looking at the tongue, &c. An eminent court-physician, visiting a noble lady from whose family he had received many shining marks of liberality and confidence, the following scene took place:—"Pray, doctor, do you think I might now venture on a slice of chicken, and a single glass of Madeira, as I feel very faint and low." "Most certainly, please your ladyship; I perceive nothing in the state of your pulse, or the appearance of your tongue, to forbid so reasonable an indulgence." Her ladyship instantly rang the bell, and with more than usual peremptoriness of manner, desired the servant to order Sir ——'s carriage; then turning to the doctor, she addressed him nearly as follows:—"Sir, there is your fee, and, depend upon it, it is the last you shall receive from me, or from any of my connexions with whom I possess any influence. I asked you a question, a serious question, sir, to me, considering the very abstemious regimen to which I have so long submitted under your direction; and I think it full time to withdraw my confidence from a physician who delivers a professional opinion without any foundation; for, sir, you must be perfectly aware that you neither felt my pulse, nor examined my tongue."

In your instructions to your patients, be particular in giving minute directions concerning diet. This has great effect on the minds of old women, especially if their maladies are, in a great measure, imaginary. Give a list of what is to be eaten at breakfast, dinner, and supper; and you may depend upon being often made the subject of conversation, and you will be considered a very "clever doctor." A physician, in large practice, brought himself into notice, by always recommending the *left leg* of a boiled fowl; and upon our attempting to persuade the invalid that the left leg possessed no peculiar virtue, she was quite indignant, and exclaimed, that "so sensible a physician must know better than you!" If you can make yourself talked about, you need have little to fear. You must not be over-scrupulous or fastidious in having recourse to this professional charlatanism. If you depend solely upon your medical knowledge, judgment, and experience, how fearful will be the opposition with which you will have to struggle! Where one man of sterling ability succeeds in practice, ten of the most shallow pretensions obtain the confidence and smiles of the discerning public. Alas! how frail and fragile are all our hopes and aspirations!

A physician who is able to drive his carriage, is considered extremely clever in his profession, and is patronized accordingly. A peer labouring under a severe fit of the gout, had a surgeon warmly recommended to him by some friends, as possessing a specific for his complaint. In compliance with this recommendation, he sent for him. On the medical man being announced, his lordship demanded of his servant, "Does this famous doctor come on foot, or in his carriage?" "On foot," was the reply. "Send the scoundrel about his business. Did he possess the secret which he pretends to have, he would ride in his coach and six, and I should have been happy to have entreated him to deliver me from this terrible disease."

It is a great point gained if you can visit the opera frequently ; and be sure to instruct the messengers, when the performance is over, to vociferate loudly for your carriage. This is an effectual way of making you known, as a London physician and a man of fashion. Be regular in your attendance at church ; and instruct your servant to call you out occasionally during the service. When you first start in practice, it will be of service if you can persuade your *carriage friends* to call often at your house. Always contrive to have a coach standing at your door on Sunday, as it is sure to attract the notice of the people as they return home from church, and will lead the public to believe that you are a practising physician.

> " For sure the pleasure is as great
> Of being cheated, as to cheat."

It is important to belong to, and speak at, the principal medical societies ; particularly if the proceedings are reported in the daily or weekly journals.

The following advice to a young London physician, on the art of getting into practice, was written by the celebrated Dr. Mead :—

" That which gives me great hopes of you (Dr, Timothy Vanbustle, M.D.) is your resolution to go on, and to push into practice at all hazards. Monsieur De Rochf observes, that there is nothing impossible if we have but the resolution to take the right way to it. Besides, you know *audaces fortuna juvat ;* and, therefore, above all things, let me as a friend advise you to take care of studying or endeavouring to know much in this way, since that will render you timorous and cautious, and consequently keep you back in your practice ; besides that, the more you search the less you will be satisfied ; and when arrived at the top of all, you may with Solon conclude, that all your wisdom (comparatively with real knowledge) is in knowing nothing. Whereas, if you only *skim* the surface, you

will go boldly on, and fancy your knowledge ten times
more than what it really is. Thus then the great and
principal thing you ought to be qualified with, is the *for-
mula prescribendi;* for form is now the main chance,
whether in law or physic; and without that, there is
nothing to be done; this is the business, the *Alpha* and
Omega, the all in all; some will succeed, and some won't;
'tis hit or miss, luck's all; you are paid, go which way
you will. And now you are just arrived in town, without
having had the benefit of establishing an acquaintance at
Oxford or Cambridge, among the nobility, clergy, &c., and
an absolute stranger here, without the assistance of dissenting teachers, relations, old women, nurses, children,
or apothecaries; the first thing I advise you to do, is to
make all the noise and bustle you can, to make the whole
town ring of you, if possible; so that every one in it may
know that there is such a being, and here in town, too,
such a physician. It signifies little which way it be done,
so that it be done, and that your name be known and heard
of, for that is half in half, since no one sends to consult
him they have not heard of, that being a crime sufficient
not to have been talked of; whereas, if accustomed to
your name, you are a fit person to be called to the sick.
Thus the famous R———f,* 'tis said, on his first arrival,
had half the porters in town employed to call for him, at
all the coffee-houses and public places, so that his name
might be known. A very famous oculist has likewise
freely told me that he must starve, did he not frequently
put himself in the public prints: but this is not so fashionable with physicians, ready to their company, or that
which they think their company understands the best, or
are otherwise so complaisant, as to talk to their friends of
their interest; for I would suppose you have insinuated
yourself into their friendship. Besides that, the very

---

* Radcliffe, we suppose.

seeing you now and then, might put them in mind of that which they might otherwise forget. The old and the simple, the riotous, the whimsical, and the fearful, are your most proper company, and who will provide you with most business; there being far less to be got by the wise and sober, who are much more rarely ailing. But then you will, perhaps, tell me, that such like physicians will be the most proper to please and keep company with such, since *similis, simili gaudet.* If so, then I can only say, that those probably will stand the fairest for business; and if you are so wise or unwise, as not to ply, bend, truckle to their humours, I doubt you will be in danger of having less business: or, otherwise, if you would still continue, and be esteemed very wise, sober, and grave, you should then learn most obsequiously to fawn and sooth man, woman, and child, since few else will thrive well, unless blessed with wit, in which case, they may be allowed a little more liberty. To make yourself known, the making friends for some public lectureship is not amiss, which serves for a feather in your cap, by which you become known, and so taken notice of as a fine fellow; and then you have an opportunity of haranguing your auditory, which, though it should be mobbish or trifling, you gain your point. As to what you read or say, it matters not much; if from the more musty and ancient authors the better; if from the more modern, the more fashionable it will be: and thus consequently you will either be esteemed a very learned, or at least a very ingenious man. If you can be introduced to an hospital, your business is done for life, be your success what it will. If your wife should happen to mind business in her way, it will certainly also increase yours, for many good reasons, as increasing your friends and acquaintances. It will not be amiss to set up an equipage, to purchase a mountain of books, and add any thing by which you will acquire the reputation of being a learned and ingenious gentleman. Let your religious and political opinions swim with the tide, especially when fashionable. Let not your fingers be sacrilegiously defiled; but be very gentle in taking fees of the clergy, &c.—People are generally employed in proportion to the manner they live in, especially if once a little known; for the employing of many artificers and tradesmen, &c., you may not only become more known, but they also support and employ you. Thus, if you get much, you must spend much; and if you spend much, you will readily get much, particularly if spent in a proper way, and once a little known. *Don Quevedo* is of opinion, that the best way to run into business is to run into debt, because your creditors will employ you to get paid:—as to putting this experiment in practice, I shall rather choose to leave it to your own natural genius to direct you therein, than much to persuade you thereto, since there may be danger, should it not succeed.

" To these hints I must observe to you, that dancing and dressing well, are not such slight accomplishments to introduce a young physician into practice, as you may imagine, because it makes him acceptable to the ladies and *beau monde:* his fashionable gesture, and gentle manner of feeling a pulse agreeably, is half the business; nay, that, and very little else may, in time, for ought I know, go a great way towards an hospital, or other public employ. In fine, I shall now leave you; may you live and brush on, so you may take the other ways to it.

" I could mention you some, who got into business in physic, by writing poetry, some by divinity, others by politics, &c. But should you have an itching to make your name known by writing a book on physic, yet so customary, I would advise you to choose the subject by which you think you will get most money, or that which will bring you the most general business, as fevers, small-pox, &c. For in those, some must always live, some die, 'tis a hard matter to tell when right, or when wrong; write which way you will, 'tis disputable; but, certain it is, that the world in general readily conclude that you certainly understand that which you write about. The method of writing, if in your frontispiece you address not your book to some great man, is to club with some other physicians; and thus by way of letters, to commend each other's good practice, and to support and make each other famous. But above all things, take particular care, let the subject be what it will, that the words be well chosen, so as to make an elegant and florid speech; since you have ten to one that mind the language more than the ideas, as Mr. Pope says :—

'Others for language all their care express,
   And value books, as women men for dress;
   Their praise is still—' the style is excellent;'
   The sense they humbly take upon content.'

"And next, then, I would advise you, whatever the subject be you write upon (if uncommon the better), rather to write, so as that no man can make any thing of it, so as neither to make downright sense, or nonsense thereof, than otherwise; because thus none of the profession can well lay hold of you for any particular part; or, if they should, there is room for you to defend it, being as easy to be understood one way as t'other. This is that method I commend, which Mr. Locke observes to be possible enough, for one to write a tolerable discourse of well-chosen and well-joined words, which, nevertheless on the whole, makes not up any real sense, or intelligible meaning. Thus I will suppose a man to write of sleep; now if I wrote in this manner, it is ten to one but that it will make all who read it fall asleep, and, consequently, what can be better said on this subject.

"The last thing I advise you to do, is to get acquainted and cheerfully to keep company with old women, midwives, nurses, and apothecaries, since these will still be entertaining you in the way of your business, and as the old ladies, &c., are most subject to ailings, so they will still be acquainting you with the same; and consequently, you are to make the most of it, and never to neglect or make slight of the least complaint; and thus you will gain the reputation of being both careful and skilful; whereas otherwise your care and skill may be suspected as well as your affectation."

Thus Dr. Mead concludes his advice to his brother physician. We do not quote it as an example for imitation, but as a curious record of the state of the profession in his day. We feel assured that no man of a properly constituted mind would have recourse to such illegitimate means of advancing himself in the world. He would rather adopt the following sentiment of Pope :—

> " But if the purchase cost so dear a price,
>   As soothing folly or exalting vice ;
>   Then teach me, Heaven ! to scorn the guilty bays,
>   Drive from my breast that wretched lust of praise ;
>   Unblemish'd let me live, or die unknown,
>   Oh, grant an *honest* fame, or grant me none."

CHAPTER V.

CHRONICLES OF WARWICK HALL; OR, MEDICAL AND SURGICAL LUMINARIES OF THE OLDEN TIME.

History of the old College of Physicians—Sir J. Cutler—Sir Charles Scarborough—Dr. Sermon—Dr. Thomas Willis—Sir. W. Petty—Dr. Gideon Harvey—Dr. Mead—An account of his Rise in Physic—Queen Caroline—Mead's Converzationes—Dr. Cadogan—Dr. J. Bainbridge—Dr. J. Fothergill—Dr. Battie—Dr. M. Baillie—Dr. Sydenham—Sir Hans Sloane—Dr W. Hunter—Dr. Hawes—Dr. Glover—Dr. G. Fordyce—Dr. Cheyne—Dr. W. Harvey—Dr. Friend—Dr. Arbuthnot—Dr. Jenner—Dr. Gregory—Dr. Lettsom—Dr. Mounsey—Sir R. Croft—Dr. Mackintosh—Sir D. Barry—Chesselden—Mr. P. Pott—Mr. Hey—Mr. Heaviside.

WHAT a myriad of pleasing and melancholy associations crowd upon our mind, as we gaze at the old College of Physicians, in Warwick Lane!

The contiguity of this College to the Old Baily, and the impression excited in the mind by a view of the entrance porch, are thus humorously alluded to by Sir Samuel Garth, in the opening canto of his " Dispensary :"—

" Not far from that most celebrated place,
    Where angry Justice shows her awful face,
    Where little villains must submit to fate,
    That great ones may enjoy the world in state,—
    There stands a dome, majestic to the sight,
    And sumptuous arches bear its awful height;
    A golden globe, placed high with artful skill,
    Seems to the distant sight a gilded pill."

We have previously stated that the College of Physicians was founded by Linacre, in the year 1518. Prior to that event, the state of medical science was very low in England. It was only remarkable for ingenious hypotheses, unsupported by the evidence of facts, and for a credulous faith in astrological influence, equally visionary. The sweating sickness raged in London with great violence previous to the year 1518. The infected died within three hours after the appearance of the disease, and no *effectual* remedy was discovered. The administration of justice was suspended during its continuance, and the court removed from place to place with precipitation and fear.

Half the people in some parts of the country were swept away, and the principal trade carried on was in coffins and shrouds; but even that, in the progress of the plague, was generally abandoned. In London, vast sepulchral pits were prepared every morning, into which the victims were thrown promiscuously. The only sounds in the city during the day, where the doleful monotony of unceasing knells, and the lamentations of the tainted, deserted by their friends, crying from the windows to the passengers to pray for them. The doors of almost every house was marked with a red cross, the sign that the destroying angel had been there; and all night, as the loaded wheels of the death-wagons rolled along, a continual cry was heard of " Bring out your dead." To discover a remedy, or some mode of averting the recurrence of this terrible calamity, the king, at the suggestion of Dr. Linacre, was induced to establish the College of Physicians: among others mentioned in the charter, as the advisers of this beneficial institution, Cardinal Wolsey's name is particularly mentioned.*

Previously to the reign of Henry the Eighth, there were but few restraints on the practice of Physic and Surgery;

---

* Vide Galt's Life of Cardinal Wolsey.

and the most illiterate and ignorant pretended to professional knowledge, and exercised the art of *killing* with
impunity. At length, in 1511, an Act of Parliament was
passed to restrict, " within the City of London, or within
seven miles of the same," the practice of either faculty
to those who should be " examined, approved of, and
admitted," by the Bishop of London, or the Dean of St.
Paul's, assisted by four doctors of Physic, and " other persons expert in surgery.*

The good effects of this act were soon apparent; and
in order to extend and perpetuate its beneficial results,
the King, on the 23d of September, 1518, instituted the
College of Physicians, by his letters patent, granted to
several persons therein named, who were incorporated
into one body, with power to form " a perpetual Com-
monalty, or Fellowship, of the Faculty of Physic."

About four years afterwards, the privileges conferred by
the charter were confirmed and extended by Parliament;
and the President, and three *Elects*, (of whom eight were
to be appointed annually,) were empowered to examine
all Physicians within the several dioceses of England, except graduates of the two Universities.—The low state of
anatomy in Queen Elizabeth's reign, may be estimated

---

* In the preamble to this act, we have the curious information, that " the science and cunning of physic and
surgery" was daily exercised by " a great multitude of
ignorant persons, of whom the greater part have no
manner of insight in the same, nor in any other kind of
learning (some, also, *can read no letters on the book*) so
far forth, that common artificers, as *smiths, weavers,* and
women, boldly, and accustomably took upon them great
cures, and things of great difficulty, in which they partly
used *sorceries* and *witchcraft,* and partly applied such
medicines unto the diseased as are very noisome, and
nothing meet therefore; to the high displeasure of God,
&c., and *destruction* of many of the King's liege people."

from the fact of that Princess having, in 1565, granted to the College the privilege " to take yearly, for ever, one, two, three, or four human bodies, to dissect and anatomize, having been condemned and dead."—Additional charters, both confirmatory and extensional, have been granted by different sovereigns; and the Society now consists of a President, Electors, Fellows, Honorary Fellows, Candidates, and Licentiates.

The first *Edifice*, wherein the College meetings were held, was given to the Society by the far-famed Dr. Linacre, who had been physician to Henry VII. and his sons Prince Arthur and Henry VIII. It had been his own habitation, and stood in *Knight-Rider Street ;* he died in 1524. In the following century, the members removed to *Amen Corner*, Paternoster Row, where they had bought some leasehold premises. Here the learned Dr. Harvey (discoverer of the circulation of the blood) erected a Convocation-room, and a Museum in the garden ; and on the Society placing his bust in their Hall, with a suitable inscription recording his discoveries, he gave the whole to the College, in the year 1652, at a splendid entertainment, to which he had invited all the members. He also, in 1656, instituted an *anniversary feast*, and at the first banquet, assigned his paternal estate, (which was of the then yearly value of £56) to the Society; partly to defray the expenses of the feast, and partly to establish an annual Latin oration.

After the destruction of the College building, in the conflagration of 1666, the Society purchased an extensive plot of ground in *Warwick Lane*, on which the present edifice was erected between the years 1674 and 1689 ; from the designs and under the superintendence of Sir Christopher Wren.*

---

* The following singular particulars relating to this pile, and to the placing of the statue of Sir John Cutler (whom Pope's caustic Satires have " damned to everlast-

The ground-plan of this building is irregular and peculiar : the buildings surround a quadrangular court, but there is a considerable difference in the measurements

---

ing fame ;" though probably to the poet's own disgrace, if the subject were thoroughly investigated,) in front of the College Theatre, within the inclosed court, are given by Pennant, from the information of Dr. Warren :—

"It also appears, by the annals of the Society, that in the year 1674, a considerable sum of money had been subscribed by the Fellows for the erection of a new College. It also appears, that Sir John Cutler, a near relation of Dr. Whistler, the President, was desirous of becoming a benefactor. A committee was appointed to wait upon Sir John, and thank him for his kind intentions : he accepted their thanks, renewed his promise, and specified that part of the building of which he intended to bear the expense. In the year 1680, statues in honour of the King and Sir John were voted by the members; and nine years afterwards, the College being then completed, it was resolved to borrow money of Sir John to discharge the College debt, but the sum is not specified. It appears, however, that in 1699, Sir John's executors made a demand on the College of £7000, which sum was supposed to include the money actually lent, the money pretended *to be given*, but set down as a *debt* in Sir John's books, and the interest on *both*. Lord Radnor, however, and Mr. Boulter, Sir John Cutler's executors, were prevailed on to accept £2000 from the College, and actually remitted the other £5000 : so that Sir John's promise, which he never performed, obtained him the statue, and the liberality of his executors has kept it in its place ever since ; but the College have wisely obliterated the inscription, which in the warmth of its gratitude, it had placed beneath the figure :—'*Omnis Cutleri cedat labor Amphitheatro.*' "—Vide Pennant's " London," p. 310, 4th edit. 1805.

of the north and south sides, although the fronts are nearly uniform. This variation arose from the confined situation and limited extent of the area on which the college was erected. The entrance in Warwick Lane, though of bold proportions and lofty elevation, cannot be seen from any point favourable to its architectural character.—An octangular porch, forty feet in diameter, and of considerable height, with a few adjoining apartments, form the eastern front of this fabric. The lofty arch of entrance, which has ponderous iron gates, is flanked by two Ionic three-quarter columns on each side, the capitals of which are enriched by festoons, and sustain a pediment and attic of the Corinthian order. The porch is surmounted by a cupola, or dome (crowned by a gilt ball) which includes the *theatre*, where chirurgical operations were formerly performed, and lectures and orations delivered.

On the inner side, three open arches lead into the quadrangular court: the buildings are of brick, having stone dressings and enrichments. The principal front, which faces the entrance, consists of two stories, Ionic below, and Corinthian above, with their respective entablatures supported by pilasters, and crowned by an angular pediment. Over the doorway is the following inscription :—" *Utriusque fortunæ exemplar ingens adversus rebus Deum probavit prosperis seipsum Collegii hujusce stator ;*" and in a rusticated niche above, formed in the centre of the second story, is a statue of King Charles II. The statue of Sir John Cutler stands on the opposite side of the court, within a niche in front of the theatre, in the upper story of the porch. The hall or court-room, is of considerable length, and well lighted on both sides by large semicircular headed windows. The ceiling is slightly coved, and much embellished with stuccoed ornaments. An open yard, or area, extends on the west side, the entire length of the building, and is skirted by the stone walls of Newgate.

After the removal of the Society to their splendid *new College*, in Pall-Mall East, on the 25th June, 1825, these premises were for some time occupied by the *self*-named "*Equitable* Loan Company." The venerable Hall is now desecrated by being turned into a butcher's market.*

In bringing before the notice of our readers sketches of some of the principal physicians of eminence whose genius immortalized the College, we would premise that it is not our intention to enter into a minute detail of their professional career—such a course would be inconsistent with the design of this work. Of many celebrated physicians little has been recorded. We have, however, endeavoured to supply, to a certain extent, the deficiency in medical biography of which we complain, imperfect as we feel our readers will think it to be.

The chief advantage of biography is, that it affords both examples for imitation, and beacons for warning. In tracing the lives of some of our most eminent physicians, the youthful student will see that it was to their industry, their zeal, their learning, their perseverance, that they owed their success, as much—if not in truth more—than to their natural endowments. We do not say that for these great men nature had done nothing, but we do say that nature did nothing for them in comparison with what they did for themselves. And

"If past experience may attain,
To something like prophetic strain,"

We may reasonably predicate of all who place before their eyes, as models for imitation, those eminent individuals who have excelled in that branch of science to which they propose to devote themselves, that a similar success, and a similar reputation will crown *their* efforts and reward *their* exertions. It is then chiefly for the

---

* Vide Mr. E. W. Brayley's "Londiniana," vol. iv.

purpose of encouraging the student about to enter upon the toilsome and perilous paths of medical practice, that these pages have been written; but we trust also that they will not be found destitute of interest or value in the eyes of the non-professional public. The moral they convey is of universal application—the truths they teach of universal importance; and we are well assured that this moral and these truths can be in no better way conveyed or enforced, than in portraying the early struggles and ultimate triumph of great men, in whatever pursuits they may be occupied.

> " Whose lives more than preceptive wisdom taught,
> The great in action, and the pure in thought."

DR. SCARBOROUGH, or SIR CHARLES SCARBOROUGH, was first physician to Charles II., James II., and William III. Mr. Oughted informs us that his memory was so tenacious, that he could recite in order all the propositions of Euclid, Archimedes, and other ancient mathematicians. He assisted Harvey in his book " De Generatione Animalium," and succeeded him as a lecturer of anatomy and surgery. He was a man of amiable manners, and of great pleasantry in conversation. Seeing the Duchess of Portsmouth eating to excess, he said to her with his usual frankness, " Madam, I will deal with you as a physician should do; *you must eat less, use more exercise, take physic, or be sick.*"

WILLIAM SERMON was an eminent physician of Bristol. He was said to have possessed a palliative remedy for the dropsy, by which the Duke of Albemarle was greatly relieved: but he not long after relapsed into this distemper, which at length proved fatal to him. Dr. Sermon, who was naturally vain, grew vainer than ever upon his success, and seemed to think nothing beyond the reach of his skill; as if a man that cured the Great Monck of the dropsy, could do every thing in the power of physic.

" Let Zoilists laugh at what is past and done,
Brave Sermon's acts shall live in face o' the sun,
Great Monck, restorer of his country's peace,
Declares from him his dropsy soon shall cease."

DR. THOMAS WILLIS was an eminent physician, who flourished in the year 1685. He was a great scholar, and wrote the Latin language with great purity. His works were much celebrated at home and abroad, and his practice was in proportion to his fame. He was regular in his devotions, his studies, and visiting his patients; and his custom was to dedicate his Sunday fees to the relief of the poor. Willis and Lower first recommended the waters of Astrop, which were afterwards decried by the celebrated Dr. Radcliffe; the reason for which was, the circumstance of the people of the village insisting upon the doctor keeping an illegitimate child, which was laid to him by an infamous woman of that place: upon this, the doctor declared "that he would put a toad into their well," and accordingly cried down the waters, which soon lost their reputation.

SIR WILLIAM PETTY was professor of anatomy in Oxford, and fellow of the College of Physicians, in the reign of Charles II. He gave early proofs of that comprehensive and inquisitive genius, for which he was afterwards so eminent; and which seems to have been designed by nature for every branch of science to which he applied himself. At the age of fifteen, he was master of all the learned languages, mathematics, geometry, navigation, &c. He made his way in the world under great disadvantages, in point of circumstances, having acquired a very moderate fortune with as much difficulty, as he afterwards rose to wealth and eminence. During a visit to France, he told Mr. Aubrey that he had lived for a week on three pennyworth of walnuts. But he at length, to use his own expression, " hewed out his fortune himself." He was an able mathematician, was skilful in drawing, and understood the practical parts of mechanics, and was an exact surveyor. He died in 1685-7.

About the same period, flourished DR. GIDEON HARVEY. There was, perhaps, never any thing more remarkable than the fortune of this man. About the latter end of King William's reign, there was a great debate who should succeed the deceased physician to the Tower. The contending parties were so equally matched in their interests and pretensions, that it was extremely difficult to determine which should have the preference. The matter was at length brought to a compromise; and Dr. Gideon Harvey was promoted to that office; for the same reason that Sixtus V. was advanced to the pontificate; because he was in appearance, sickly and infirm; and his death was expected in a few months. He, however, survived not only his rivals, but all his contemporary physicians; and died after he had enjoyed his sinecure above fifty years.

In the year 1696 lived the celebrated Dr. Mead, the origin of whose success, as a physician, we have recorded in our sketch of his illustrious contemporary, Radcliffe. According to another authority, Mead's rise in life was owing to his being called in to a celebrated Duchess, distinguished for her intemperate propensities. The Doctor had sacrificed rather more freely to the jolly god than was consistent with a healthy exercise of his faculties, and, as he was feeling his patient's pulse, his foot slipped, when he ejaculated—" Drunk !—yes, quite drunk !" alluding to himself. The Duchess, imagining he had found out her complaint, which she was most anxious to conceal, told Mead, if he kept her secret, she would recommend him. He did so, and the Doctor rose to fame and opulence.

Notwithstanding the violence displayed by Dr. Mead, in his controversy with Woodward, whom it is represented he challenged, and compelled to beg pardon,* he was, in his general conduct, mild and forbearing. On one occasion, a servant, whom he asked to look for his spectacles, told him petulantly, but without exciting any observation in reply, that " he was always losing his things." His anger was, however, occasionally roused. He once said to a divine, who, instead of attending to his prescriptions, had been following the directions laid down by Dr. Cheyne—"Sir, I have never yet, in the whole course of my practice, taken or demanded a fee of a clergyman ; but, since you have pleased, contrary to what I have met with in any other gentleman of your profession, to prescribe to me, rather than follow my prescriptions, when you had committed the care of your recovery to my skill and trust, you must not take it amiss, nor will, I hope, think it unfair, if I demand ten guineas of you." The clergyman paid the money, six guineas of which Mead subsequently returned.

---

* A different version is, however, given of this altercation. It is said that Mead and Woodward met, and both drew, and that Mead, not loving cold iron, retreated ; when Woodward, making a false step, fell down. His antagonist then ran in, and, standing over him, demanded if he would submit and ask his life. " If you threatened me with your *physic*, I might beg my life," said Woodward, " but I certainly shall not ask it for fear of your sword." Among the prints which adorn Ward's "Lives of the Gresham Professors," is a gateway, entering from Broad-street, marked 25. Within are figures of two persons, the one standing, and the other kneeling. These represent Dr. Woodward, the Professor of Physic, and Mead ; and allude to the transaction referred to above :—

" Physicians, if they're wise, should never think,
    Of any arms but such as pen and ink."
                                        GARTH.

Another anecdote is recorded of this celebrated physician, but we have some doubts whether Dr. Mead was
the "happy man" referred to. We give it, however, as
we find it narrated. Mead lived on terms of intimacy
with a clergyman in his neighbourhood. The former was
attacked with a fit of the gout, when Mead attended him,
of course, gratuitously, and cured him. Some time after
this, Mead called upon the clergyman to ask him to perform the matrimonial service, and the call was cheerfully
obeyed. After the performance of the nuptial ceremony,
the clergyman, unobserved, made his escape, and Mead's
brother followed him to his house, and offered him a
handsome fee. The divine, it is said, retired for a few
minutes to his study, and returned the fee to the bearer,
with the following impromptu :—

"To the Doctor the Parson's a sort of a brother,
And a good turn from one deserves one from the other;
So take back your guineas, dear doctor, again;
Nor give—what you so well can remedy—*pain.*
Permit me to wish you all joy and delight,
On th' occasion that brought us together to-night;
May health, wealth, and fame, attend you thro' life,
And every day add to the bliss of your *wife!*"

Mead dabbled considerably in the stocks. One day,
prior to his visiting his patients, he received intelligence
that the stocks had suddenly fallen. At this moment he
was sent for, in a great hurry, to visit a lady who was
represented to be very ill. Having considerable property
in the funds, the news made so strong an impression upon
his mind, that, whilst he was feeling the patient's pulse,
he exclaimed, "Mercy upon me, how they fall! lower!
lower! lower!" The lady, in alarm, flew to the bell,
crying out, "I am dying! Dr. Mead says, my pulse gets
lower, and lower; so that it is impossible I should live!"
"You are dreaming, madam," replied the physician, rous-

ing himself from his reverie; "your pulse is very good, and nothing ails you: it was the stocks I was talking of."

Dr. Wharton, in his life of the Duke of Marlborough, says, in his last illness Dr. Mead was consulted. When the physician had given his instructions and written his prescription, he left the chamber; the Duchess, not liking the advice he had given, followed him to the door, and would, had she not been prevented, have torn off his periwig.

Dr. Friend's practice was principally confined to the members of the high church or tory party; Mead was patronized by the Whigs. When Dr. Friend was confined, during the suspension of the Habeas Corpus Act, under a suspicion of being concerned in a plot for the restoration of the Stuarts, Mead was incessant in his endeavours to obtain his liberation. At length, being called to attend Sir Robert Walpole, he absolutely refused to prescribe for him unless Friend was released, and he succeeded in effecting his object.

A large party assembled at Mead's in the evening, to congratulate Friend; and, upon his retiring with Arbuthnot, Mead took Friend into his closet, and there put into his hands a bag containing all the fees he had received from Friend's patients during his confinement, amounting to no less than 5,000 guineas.

Friend once received a fee of 300 guineas for a journey from London to Ingestree, in Staffordshire, to attend Mr. Pulteny, who lay there dangerously ill, but recovered before Friend arrived.

During almost half a century Dr. Mead was at the head of his profession; which brought him in, one year, upwards of 7,000*l.*, and between 5,000*l.* and 6,000*l.* for several years. The clergy, and, in general, all men of learning, were welcome to his advice; and his doors were open every morning to the most indigent, whom he frequently assisted with money; so that, notwithstanding his

great genius, he did not die rich. He was a most generous patron of learning and learned men, in all sciences,
and in every country ; by the peculiar munificence of his
disposition, making the private gains of his profession
answer the end of a princely fortune, and valuing them
only as they enabled him to become more extensively useful, and thereby to satisfy the greatness of his mind,
which will transmit his name to posterity with a lustre
not inferior to that which attends the most distinguished
characters of antiquity.

No foreigner of any learning, taste, or even curiosity,
ever came to England without being introduced to Dr.
Mead ; and he was continually consulted in difficult cases
by eminent continental physicians. His large and spa-
cious house, in Great Ormond-street, became a repository
of all that was curious in nature or in art, to which his
extensive correspondence with the learned in all parts of
Europe, not a little contributed. The King of Naples
sent to request a copy of all his works. The King of
France did him the same honour. Dr. Mead's library
consisted of 10,000 volumes. His pictures, after his
death, sold for 3,417l. 11s.

A gentleman, who was troubled with a constant affection of his eyes, waited on Dr. Mead for advice. The
doctor desired him to leave off drinking wine. In a few
weeks the patient felt the good effects of the prescription,
and waited on the doctor to thank him for his advice.
He was not a little surprised to find him in a tavern, dis-
cussing a bottle of wine with a friend. " Well," said the
patient, " I see you doctors do not follow your own prescriptions." To which Mead replied, " if you love your
eyes better than wine, don't drink it ; but, as I love wine
better than my eyes, I do drink it."

Mead, calling one day on a gentleman who had been
severely afflicted with the gout, found, to his surprise,
the disease gone, and the patient rejoicing on his recovery
over a bottle of wine. " Come along, doctor," exclaimed

the patient, "you are just in time to taste this bottle of Madeira; it is the first of a pipe that has just been broached." "Ah!" replied Mead, "these pipes of Madeira will never do; they are the cause of all your suffering." "Well, then," rejoined the gay incurable, "fill your glass, for now we have found out *the cause*, the sooner we get rid of it the better."

Walpole says, that Lady Sandon's influence over Queen Caroline arose from her being possessed of the secret of her Majesty's being afflicted with *hernia umbilicus*. This, from motives of delicacy, she had communicated to the mistress of the robes, Lady Sandon: she was even so imprudent as to conceal her disease from the medical men, who treated her for gout of the stomach. When the danger became imminent, concealment was impossible.

Dr. Sands suggested that a cure might be effected by the injection of warm water. Dr. Mead entered a most positive protest against the experiment. Sir Edward Hulse was the only court physician who approved of the operation. At the time when the operation was performed, every wish to keep her Majesty's malady a secret must have been abandoned: for the courtiers, both male and female, were assembled in the anti-chamber, waiting anxiously the event.

The intestine was burst in the operation, and Dr. Sands and Sir Edward Hulse saw that the Queen must inevitably die of mortification within a few hours. The only question which then remained for the two physicians to consider was, how they might get out of the palace before the unfortunate issue was known. They determined to say that the operation had succeeded. As soon as the two physicians came out of the Queen's chamber, and announced their success, the old Duke of Newcastle, who was among those who waited in the anti-chamber, ran up to Dr. Sands, and hugged him, exclaiming, "You dear creature, the nation can never sufficiently reward you for having saved the life of the most valuable woman in the world!" The doctor struggled to get away, apprehensive that some of the ladies, who had gone into the Queen after the physicians had left her, might come out and disclose the truth.*

Mead rendered himself celebrated for his *conversaziones*, to which he invited the great wits and literati of the day. The following allusion to these interesting meetings occurs in a popular work of the present day:—

"Pray doctor," said the Counsellor —————, "what a pity it is, methinks, we have so few of these *conversaziones* now-a-days—they are so rational, so delightful. I remember, when a boy, how much I wished to be a man, that I might be permitted to join the societies of this caste. There were I know not how many in the neighbourhood of my poor father, in Ormond Street. First, I recollect Sir Hans Sloane's, in Bloomsbury Square—ha!—ha!—ha!—the precise old gentleman; he used to be so out of temper when they spilled the coffee on his carpets; and that reminds me of Handel, whom I can well recollect. He was there one evening (as I heard him relate) and inadvertently laid his muffin on one of the old Knight's books. 'To be sure it was a *gareless* trick,' said the great composer, 'but it *tid no monsdrous mischief*; *pode it put the old poog-vorm treadfully out of sorts*. I offered my best apologies,' said he, 'but the old miser would not have done with it.'—'It is really a want of feeling to do these things,' said Sir Hans. 'If it had been a biscuit, it would not have mattered; but muffin and butter—only think, Mr. Martin Folkes!'"

"'*Ah,—that is the rub!*' (said Handel,) '*it is the pudder!* now, mine worthy friend, Sir Hans Sloane, you have a *nodable excuse*—you may save your *doast* and *pudder*, and lay it to dat unfeeling gòrmandizing Ger-

---

* Nichol's "Recollections of Geo. III.," vol. i. p. 369, and Cox's "Life of Walpole."

man; and den I knows it will add something to your life, by sparing your *burse !*"

" I have been told every one enjoyed this blunt humour of Handel's; for Sir Hans, although a very good man in most respects, was parsimonious to a great fault. Indeed, it was said, on Sir Hans discontinuing these meetings, which had for a long time drawn a select number of distinguished men together on a winter's night, that it was principally to save his tea and bread and butter.

" Not so with Dr. Mead. What a princely mind had that noble creature! I can remember his benignant look when once I was taken to him by my father—it was one forenoon—to see his fine collection of paintings. I could not be more than eight or nine years old, yet I well remember a formal beau of the old school being there, who was talking very pompously about the pictures. This was Master' Aaron Hill. Yes, I remember him the rather, because, little urchin as I was, I observed to my father, when we left the Doctor's, on his asking me, with fond condescension, how I liked what I had seen—' Sir, I think Mr. Aaron Hill was very rude to talk as he did about Dr. Mead's picture; and if I had been the Doctor, I would have caned him.' Sirs, my father laughed at my *manikin* expression all the way home. And that, too, reminds me of my poor father's humour for some years after; for when my eldest brothers used to have any little dispute with me, the worthy old gentleman used to say, ' Take care, masters, or you may come in for a *cane-ing.*'

" This picture relating to Aaron Hill was a clever whole-length—I say clever, though I could be no judge then, because I have lately seen it in the Foundling Hospital—was painted by my old friend Allan Ramsey. It is so like—ah, what a wonderful art !—that I could have spoken to it, it carried me so completely back to my infancy.

" Aaron, I remember, among other faults declared—

which to be sure is no small one—it was not like the
Doctor, which I thought very odd, being no connoiseur,"
added the counsellor, smiling; " for I thought it so strong
a resemblance, that I fancied it was almost alive, and
wondered how such a work could be done. He further
said to my father, 'Sir, no man can paint now, except
Mr. Reynolds—and he is not fit to hold a candle to Van-
dyke.'

" All this, boy as I was, I thought very strange and
very foolish; or perhaps," said the candid relator, with
becoming self-knowledge, " I now think so—for the story
of that visit was so often told at my father's table, that I
may give to myself the merit of reflections made by my
elders. One thing, however, I may safely say, which is,
that Master Aaron appeared to me a rude and a pedantic
coxcomb.

" That Dr. Mead was a great soul indeed !" said my
friend the Cantab. " How much more society is indebted
to such a being than the far greater part of mankind is
aware of! Here was a man who raised a fortune by his
rare talent; who, amidst the arduous labours of his professional duties, yet found leisure to cultivate his love for
the arts and sciences; who spared no expense in collecting works of taste, but moreover, who, with a munificence
and benevolence that must endear his memory to all good
men, did not this out of ostentation—no! but from the
generous desire to promote the study of polite arts at his
own expense;—urged to this act by that dignified feeling
which could not bear to behold genius disregarded, or to
think that the children of taste were the only orphans, in
an age of civilization, who were left to battle alone with
adversity. That great and good man, Sirs, when he had
formed his collection, which was certainly in those days
no mean one, threw open his gallery for the benefit of the
students in painting and sculpture, and his house on a
morning was truly an academy of science.

" Sirs, I have it on indubitable authority, that he would

lend any, even the most costly of his pictures, to any respectable artist for an exemplar ; and let us suppose what
a valuable patron such a man must have been, in such an
age of apathy to these matters as the reign of the second
George."

"In the autumn of 1738," says Dr. Cuming to Lettsom,
" I frequently visited Dr. Mead.   One morning, while at
breakfast, he told me that he had been applied to by Sir
William (then Dr. Brown), who had come to reside in the
metropolis, to recommend a physician of character to
supply his place at Lynn.   Dr. Mead obligingly told me,
that, if agreeable, he would recommend me for this purpose.   This offer I thankfully accepted of.   When I next
waited on the doctor, he acquainted me that he had, according to his promise mentioned me to Dr. Brown, but
that he, on inquiring who and what I was, objected to
me, saying, he should accept of no person as his successor, who was not a graduate of Oxford and Cambridge."   Dr. Mead, piqued at this reply, as considering
such a circumstance to be of very little importance, answered with some warmth, " Sir, you annexed no such
condition on your first application to me.   For the sake of
my own character, you might have been persuaded that I
would have recommended no gentleman to you, but one
with whom I was acquainted, who had had a liberal education, and whose manners and abilities I was well informed of by persons of credit who had introduced him
to me.   Do you, Sir, yourself look out for a successor to
your own taste ; I shall concern myself no further in this
business."   It was principally to Dr. Mead that the
several counties of England, and our Colonies abroad,
applied for the choice of their physicians, as he never recommended any but such whose capacity he was well
assured of.   He never failed to assist them with his advice and information when they had recourse to him in
difficult cases, and required nothing of them in return.

but an account of their several discoveries and observations, of which they enjoyed the whole honour.*

It has been justly said of this distinguished physician, that "of all physicians who had ever flourished, he gained the most, spent the most, and enjoyed the highest favour during his lifetime, not only in his own, but in foreign countries."†

In 1660 flourished DOCTOR CADOGAN, who was distinguished as much for his fondness for shooting, as for his medical skill. The following lines refer to this physician :—

" Doctor, all game you either ought to shun,
   Or sport no longer with the unsteady gun,
   But like physicians of undoubted skill,
   Gladly attempt what never fails to kill,   •
   Not *lead's* uncertain dross, but *physic's* deadly pill."

This physician, who was at one time in indifferent circumstances, married a rich old lady, over whose wealth he had an entire control. Like most mercantile marriages, it was not of the happiest kind. The lady had a suspicion on her mind, that the doctor would one day poison her with his physic in order to get her out of his way, and feeling ill, on one occasion, she exclaimed that she was poisoned. "Poisoned!" said the doctor to a number of his wife's friends who were present, "how can that possibly be? Whom do you accuse of the

---

* Pettigrew, vol. i. p. 103, dated March 6, 1785.

† The following lines were addressed to the author of an epitaph on Dr. Mead :—

" Mead's not dead then, you say, only sleeping a little ;
   Why, egad ! Sir, you've hit it off there to a tittle ;
   Yet, friend, his awakening I very much doubt,
   Pluto knows who he's got, and will ne'er let him out."

crime?" "You," replied the indignant wife. "Gentle-men," said the doctor, with considerable *non-chalance*, "it is perfectly false. You are quite welcome to open her at once, and you will then discover the calumny."

In the 18th century lived Dr. JOHN BAINBRIDGE, an eminent physician and astronomer. Judging from the accounts published of him, he must have ranked high as a scholar and medical philosopher. His description of the comet in 1618, made him acquainted with Sir Henry Savile, who, without any application or recommendation in favour of Dr. Bainbridge, appointed him his first pro-fessor of astronomy at Oxford, in the year 1619. He was a most voluminous writer on astronomical subjects. An odd story is related of him by Dr. Walter Pope, in his Life of Seth Ward, Bishop of Salisbury. Speaking of the doctor he says, "This is the same Dr. Bainbridge who was afterwards Savilian Professor of Astronomy at Oxford, a learned and good mathematician. Yet there goes a story of him, which was in many scholars' mouths, when I was first admitted there, that he put upon the school-gate, as the custom is, an *affiche* or written paper, giving notice at what time, and upon what subject, the professor will read, which ended in these words—*Lec-tures de polis et axis*, under which was written, by an unknown hand, as follows:—

> " Doctor Bainbridge
> Came from Cambridge,
> To read *de polis et axis:*
> Let him go back again,
> Like a dunce as he came,
> And learn a new syntaxis."

Dr. Bainbridge died the 3d of November, 1643, aged sixty-two.

DOCTOR JOHN FOTHERGILL was the son of parents who professed the principles of Quakerism. They are sup-

posed to have been in the middle rank of life, and to
have gone through the world with no other distinction in
society, than that which belonged to the humble claims
of honest industry.

To those who remember the sobriety and decorum of
Fothergill's deportment, it will appear incredible that at
any period of his life he should have acted in such a
manner as to give offence to decency and propriety ; and
were not the fact of public notoriety, and within the memory of many now living, it would hardly deserve credit,
or meet with any belief. But however extraordinary it
may appear, it is confidently asserted, that while he resided at Edinburgh he walked the length of High Street
naked to the waist, and, in a fit of inspiration, denounced
God's vengeance on the inhabitants. The motive for an
action so indecent and eccentric, sets all conjecture at
defiance.

Dr. Fothergill commenced the practice of his profession in 1740, in a house situated in White-heart Court,
Lombard Street, where he continued the greater part of
his life, and acquired and established both his fame and
fortune.

Dr. Fothergill was as distinguished for his charity, as
for his medical skill. A physician of eminence, who had
long been on a friendly footing with him, being under
difficulties, and having a wife and several children to
support, mentioned his distress to him, when, to his great
satisfaction, Dr. Fothergill presented him with a draft
upon his banker for £1000. Since his death it appears
from his memoranda, that for the last twenty-five years
his fees averaged £6700 per annum. Fothergill entertained high notions respecting the dignity of the profession he followed. Nothing (says Dr. Lettsom) hurt his
feelings more, than an estimate of the medical profession,
formed upon lucrative advantages. He was ever averse
to speak of his pecuniary emoluments. " My only wish,"
he declared, " was to do what little business might fall to

my share, as well as possible, and to banish all thoughts of practising physic as a money-getting trade, with the same solicitude as I would the suggestions of vice or intemperance." In a letter written several years afterwards, when he was in the receipt of a large professional income, he writes, " I endeavour to follow my business, because it is my duty, rather than my interest; *the last is inseparable from a just discharge of duty;* but I have ever wished to look at the profits in the last place, and this wish has attended me ever since my beginning." Again he says, " I wished most fervently, and I endeavour after it still, to do the business that occurred, with all the diligence I could, as *a present duty*, and endeavoured to repress any rising idea of *its consequences*—such a circumscribed unaspiring temper of mind, doing every thing with diligence, humility, and as in the sight of the God of healing, frees the mind from much unavailing distress and consequential disappointment."

We have already stated that charity was a predominant feature in Dr. Fothergill's character. It is stated that during the summer he retired to Lea Hall, in Cheshire. He devoted one day in every week to attendance at Middlewich, the nearest market-town, and gave his gratuitous advice to the poor. He assisted the clergy, not merely with his advice, but, on numerous occasions, with his purse. On one occasion he was reproved by a friend for his refusal of a fee from a person who had attained a high rank in the church. " I had rather (replied the doctor) return the fee of a gentleman whose rank I am not perfectly acquainted with, than run the risk of taking it from a man who ought, perhaps, to be the object of my bounty." When he paid his last visit to patients in decayed circumstances, it was not unusual with him, under the appearance of feeling the pulse, to slip into their hand a sum of money, or a bank-note. In one instance this mode of donation is said to have conveyed £150. To the modest or proud poverty which shuns the

11*

light of observation, he was the delicate and zealous visiter : in order to preclude the necessity of acknowledgment, which is often painful to such minds, he would endeavour to invent some motive for his bounty, and hence afford to the receiver the pretensions of a claim, while the liberal donor appeared to be only discharging a debt.

Lord Clive had been living for some time at Bath, under a regimen for reducing the enormous quantity of opium which he had gradually brought his constitution to bear ; and when this object was in a great degree effected, the physicians absolutely forbad his taking the waters, and advised his return to London. On his arrival there, Dr. Fothergill, whom he immediately consulted, blamed him very much for the course he had adopted, and advised his immediate return to Bath, strongly recommending the waters of that place as the only means of relief. Thus buffeted about by his different physicians, and concluding from their conduct towards him that his case would not admit of any remedy, he resolved to obviate the lingering approaches of death by the fatal application of his own hand.

A few years before the death of this celebrated physician, a Cumberland gentleman, much addicted to the bottle, and possessed of few Christian virtues, coming to town, applied to the doctor for advice. Being introduced, Fothergill, who had some knowledge of his person, which, however, he chose to conceal, inquired what was his ailment; to which the patient replied, he was very well in health, eat well, drank well, and slept well, but wished to know how he might be guarded against *sudden snaps*. The venerable physician, feeling a supreme contempt for so dissolute and abandoned a character, gave him a prescription for his *complaint* in the following deserved reproof: " *Do justice, love mercy, walk humbly with thy God, and do not snap the bottle too often.*"

Of Dr. Fothergill, Dr. Cuming observes: " He pos-

sessed a greater purity of manners, more self-govern-
ment, and a more absolute command of his passions than
any man I ever knew, who was constantly engaged in
business, and a continued intercourse with the world.
After saying thus much, I may be allowed to remark,
that there was in his manner a *perpendicularity*, a certain *formality*, and *solemnity*, which checked, in some
measure, the approach of strangers. He generally wore,
indeed, on his countenance a smile—it was a smile of
benignity and philanthropy, and to his patients it was a
hope-inspiring smile.

> " Seldom he laugh'd, and laugh'd in such a sort,
> As if he mock'd himself, and scorn'd his spirit
> That could be mov'd to laugh at any thing."

" But all this I attribute to his having been initiated
from his birth, and educated in the most rigid maxims of
the religious society to which he belonged, of the propriety of which he was thoroughly convinced, and most
strictly tenacious. Had he been a member of any other
religious sect, this formality in his manner would not
have appeared, the benevolence of his heart would have
unfurled his features, relaxed them into a careless cordi-
ality of aspect, and softened the rigour of austere virtues.
No man, I believe, that mixed with the world ever passed
through life with fewer relaxations from duty, for the
enjoyment of what is usually denominated pleasure. I
could have wished him to have been less tenacious of
some discriminating peculiarities, which in my opinion
are indifferent ; but he possessed a great degree of self-
diffidence."

At the commencement of the American war, Mr.
Grenville, then in power, wishing to know how the quaker colonists stood affected, sent a messenger to Dr. Fothergill, intimating that he was indisposed, and desiring
to see him in the evening. The doctor came, and his

patient immediately drew from him the information he
wanted on the popular topic of American affairs.   The
conversation lasted through a large portion of the evening, and it was concluded by Mr. Grenville saying, he
found himself so much better for the doctor's visit, that
he would not trouble him to prescribe.   In parting, Mr.
Grenville slipped five guineas into the doctor's hand,
which Fothergill surveying, said with a dry, arch tone,
" At *this* rate, friend, I will spare thee an hour whenever
you please to send for me !"

" I remember," says Dr. Lettsom,* " when at Lea Hall,
with Dr. Fothergill, one Sunday when the barber disappointed him, and his attendance at meeting seemed likely
to be prevented, and the doctor in the fidgets, I observed
to him : ' That his servant, Emanuel, could shave him.'
The doctor, with the fire and quickness which sometimes
overcame him, hastily replied : ' If thou mean to preserve
authority in thy house, never suffer a servant to take thee
by the nose.'   I was silent, and the barber's opportune
arrival restored placidity and good humour."

The fortune which Fothergill left was computed at
£80,000.   During the prevalence of the influenza, in the
year 1775-6, he is said to have attended sixty patients a
day, and his profits were then estimated at £8000 a year.

In the eighteenth century lived the celebrated DOCTOR
BATTIE.   He was educated at Eton ; and in 1722, he was
sent to King's College, Cambridge, where he obtained the
Craven scholarship.   The following is an account of the
doctor's mode of living, before he obtained this honour,
from the pen of one of his competitors, Dr. Morell : " We
jogged on in *statu quo*, till we came to the upper end of
the school ; when Dr. Bland introduced a new method of
declaiming (and I think a very good one) : instead of a
theme, I was to make a motion, as in the Athenian council, *Exulet Themistocles*, and Battie was to defend himself

---

* Pettigrew's Life of Dr. L. vol. i. 121.

as Themistocles. We were strictly charged to have no assistance in the composition; and as there was something in mine, with regard to the argumentative part, far above my reach, Battie every where proclaimed that it was not mine; and even Dr. Bland suspected me, till I gave him an account of the plagiarism, from a weekly paper, in one of the letters signed Cato, against affecting popularity, for which Dr. Bland blamed me."

A pretty picture Dr. Morell gives of Battie's college life. He says, "We went to King's College about the same time; and during our scholarship, Battie's mother kindly recommended us to the chandler, at 4s. 6d. *per dozen*. But, as the candles proved very dear even at that price, we resented it; and one evening getting into Battie's room before canonical hour, we locked him out, lighted and stuck up all the candles we could find in his box, round the room; and, while I thumped on the spinnet, the rest danced round me in their shirts. Upon Battie's coming, and finding what we were at, he fell to stammering and swearing till the old vice provost, Dr. Willymot, called out from above, "Who is that swearing, like a common soldier?" "It is I," quoth Battie. "Visit me," said the vice-provost, which, indeed, we were all obliged to do the next morning with a distich, according to custom. Mine naturally turned upon, "So fiddled Orpheus, and so danced the brutes;" which having explained to the vice-provost, he punished me and Sleech with a few lines of the Iliad of Homer, and Battie with the whole third book of Milton, to get, as we say, by heart. Dr. Battie belonged to Taylors' Inn, and he told me of a stranger calling him a *Taylor* in London. In his edition of Isocrates I wrote the following verses.

> "Nay, hold! friend Battie, quit the press,
>   Nor further urge the failure;
> Your author asks no better dress
>   From such a bungling taylor.

" Full happily the man mistook,
　　Unknowing of thy fame,
Who, ere you had botch'd, or patch'd a book,
　　Miscalled you by this name.

" But if this name still gives offence,
　　And 'quack' you'd rather hear,
As nothing shows a man of sense
　　Like knowing his own sphere;

" Confine yourself to license given,
　　Nor dare beyond your trade ;
Though you are free to kill the living,
　　Yet prythee spare the dead."

Dr. Battie originally intended to study law, but being disappointed in some pecuniary assistance which he expected to receive from his relations, he turned his attention to physic.

Dr. Battie commenced practice at Cambridge, but subsequently removed to Uxbridge, and then to London, where the emoluments of his practice produced him £1000 per annum.

In the year 1738, he married the daughter of the under-master of Eton School, Barnham Goode, the same person who was humoured with the following extraordinary couplet by Pope :—

" So, sneering Goode, half malice and half whim,
　　A friend in glee, ridiculously grim."

In a dispute which the College of Physicians had with Dr. Schomberg, about the year 1750, Dr. Battie, who was at that time one of the censors, took a very active part against that gentleman; and in consequence of it was thus severely characterized in a poem called " The Battiad."

" First *Battus* came, deep read in worldly art,
　　Whose tongue ne'er knew the secrets of his heart;

In mischief mighty, though but mean of size,
And, like the tempter, ever in disguise.
See him, with aspect grave, and gentle tread,
By slow degrees approach the sickly bed :
Then at his club, behold him alter'd soon,
The solemn doctor turns a low buffoon :
And he, who lately in a learned freak,
Poach'd every Lexicon, and published Greek,
Still madly emulous of vulgar praise,
From Punch's forehead wrings the dirty bays."

By successfully mimicking this character, however, he is said to have once saved a young patient's life. He was sent for to a gentleman between the age of fifteen and sixteen, who was in extreme misery from a swelling in his throat; when Dr. Battie understood what the complaint was, he opened the curtain, turned his wig and acted Punch with so much humour and success, that the lad was thrown into convulsive fits of laughter, which caused the tumour to break, and a complete cure was the consequence.

When Dr. Battie resided in the country, he affected to be his own day labourer, and to dress like one; nay, so very meanly was he attired, that one day going to visit a patient, the servant would not let him into the house; a scuffle ensued, and the doctor pushed himself into the saloon by main force.

One of Dr. Battie's whims was building. At Marlow he erected a house, forgetting to make a stair-case; and at high flood, the offices below where constantly under water. This house he lived in to his death. He insisted that the barges should be drawn up the river by horses instead of men. This, though a useful scheme, disobliged both poor and rich at the time, and a number of bargemen had very nearly tossed him over the bridge into the water. He escaped by acting Punch. From that time, for fear of future insults he always carried pocket pistols about with him.*

In 1757, he was appointed physician to St. Luke's Hospital, and he published a quarto treatise on madness; in which having thrown out some censures on the medical practice formerly used in Bethlem Hospital, he was replied to, and severely animadverted on, by Dr. J. Monro, whose father had been lightly spoken of in the treatise. Monro having humorously enough taken Horace's " *O major, tandem parcas Insane, minori,*" for the motto of his " Remarks on Battie's Treatise," the men of mirth gave him the name of Major Battie instead of doctor.

In 1776, he was seized with a paralytic stroke, which carried him off, June 13th, in the same year, in his 75th year. The night he expired, conversing with his servant, a lad who attended on him as a nurse, he said to him, " young man, you have heard, no doubt, how great are the terrors of death. This night will probably afford you some experiment; but may you learn, and may you profit by the example, that a conscientious endeavour to perform his duty through life, will ever close a Christian's eyes with comfort and tranquillity." He soon departed without a struggle or a groan. He was buried by his own direction, at Kingston, in Surrey, " as near as possible to his wife, without any monument or memorial whatever."

Doctor Mathew Baillie commenced his professional career under most favourable auspices. He was desirous of going into the church; but the eminence of his uncle, Dr. W. Hunter, induced him to study medicine. He was the son of an able professor of divinity. He married Sophia, the second daughter of the celebrated Dr. Denman. Mr. Baillie's sister was married to the late Sir Richard Croft, a man whose name is endeared in the recollections of many, as well for his manly and upright

---

* See Francis Carter's " Letter," v. iv. Nichol's Eighteenth Century," p. 607.

heart, as for his professional celebrity. Miss Joanna Baillie, who has attained so high a rank in literature, was Dr. Baillie's sister.

Under the tuition of his maternal uncle, Dr. W. Hunter, his progress was very rapid. As a specimen of the course adopted by his preceptor, in order to instil into Baillie's mind a knowledge of his profession, we give the following: "Mathew, do you know any thing of to-day's lecture?" demanded Dr. Hunter of his nephew. "Yes, sir, I hope I do." "Well then, demonstrate to me." "I will go and fetch the preparation, sir." "Oh, no matter, if you know the subject really, you will know it whether the preparation be absent or present." After this short dialogue, Dr. Hunter would stand with his back to the fire, while young Baillie demonstrated the subject of the lecture which had just been delivered; and then the student was encouraged by approbation and assistance; or immediately upon the spot, convicted of having carried away with him nothing but the loose and inaccurate information.

Of Dr. Baillie's generosity and liberality, his biographer has recorded the following instances: "A young lady who was suffering from a pulmonary complaint, asked his advice, and he recommended her to spend the winter months in a milder part of the country. He found that her circumstances would not admit of her trying this last resource to gain her health; and to enable her to do so, he instantly gave her an adequate sum of money.

The following instance came under the observation of Mr. Wardrop, and is thus recorded by him: "A lady, whose rank in life was far above her pecuniary resources, had an illness, when Dr. B.'s attendance became important, and during which he regularly took his fee, until it was no longer necessary; he then left in a bag the whole amount of what he had received, offering to the lady an apology, that he knew that had he once refused to take

his fee during his attendance, she would not have permitted him to continue it."

During the time he was spending the great part of
each week at Windsor, in attendance on the Princess
Amelia, who was then on her death-bed, so that the time
he had to spend in London was more than completely
occupied, a lady who had the dropsy, though aware of
her hopeless condition, expressed a wish, that if she could
but see Dr. Baillie, she should die contented. "I communicated to him," says Mr. Wardrop, "her wish, and he
immediately acquiesced. He interrogated her about her
means, which I knew to be very slender; he in conse-
sequence objected to take any fee, and continued punctually to visit her as long as she lived."

In 1810, Dr. B. was commanded by the late king to attend, in conjunction with Sir. H. Halford, Sir D. Dundas,
and Dr. Pope, on his youngest daughter, the Princess
Amelia. Though he was very sensible of the honour of
receiving such a command, yet he felt that it was adding
greatly to the embarrassment occasioned by his very extensive practice; but whatever might have been the inconvenience of this attendance to himself, the condescension and kindness of his late Majesty very soon recon-
ciled him to his visits at Windsor. Among other memoranda of Dr. Baillie, was found the following anecdote:
"One day when I waited on the king, with the other
medical attendants, in order to give an account of the
Princess Amelia, his Majesty said to me, 'Dr. Baillie, I
have a favour to ask of you, which I hope you will not
refuse me, it is that you will become my physician extraordinary.' I bowed, and made the best acknowledgment
in words that I could. His Majesty added, 'I thought
you would not refuse me, and therefore, I have given
directions that your appointment should be made out.'
A few days after," continues Dr. Baillie, "when we again
waited on the king, he said to the other medical men in
my presence, 'I have made Dr. Baillie my physician ex-

traordinary against his will, but not against his heart.'"
On one occasion the king was advised to go to Bath, and
Dr. B. recommended him to consult there a medical
gentleman whom he named; the king immediately con-
jectured the country from whence he came, and after
listening to all Dr. Baillie had to say to him, his Majesty
jocosely observed, "I suppose, Dr. Baillie, he is not a
Scotchman."

During Baillie's latter years, when he had retired from
all but consultation practice, and had ample time to attend to each individual case, he was very deliberate,
tolerant, and willing to listen to whatever was said to
him by the patient; but, at an earlier period, in the
hurry of great business, when his day's work, as he used
to say, amounted to sixteen hours, he was sometimes
rather irritable, and betrayed a want of temper in hearing the tiresome details of an unimportant story. After
listening, with torture, to a pressing account from a lady,
who ailed so little that she was going to the opera that
evening, he had happily escaped from the room, when he
was urgently requested to step up-stairs again; it was to
ask him whether, on her return from the opera, she
might eat some oysters. "Yes, ma'am," said Baillie,
"shells and all."

A few years ago, before Dr. Baillie's death, during a
visit which the late Professor Gregory, of Edinburgh,
made to London, these eminent physicians, equally distinguished in their separate departments, conversed together on several occasions; and the judgment they
jocosely passed upon each other, was expressed in the
following manner: "Baillie," said the accomplished and
classical professor, "knows nothing but physic." "Gregory," exclaimed the experienced and skilful London
practitioner, "seems to me to know every thing but
physic."

Baillie was rejected at the College. He called the next
day on Dr. Barrowby, who was one of the censors, and

insisted upon his fighting him. Barrowby, who was a little puny man, declined it. "I am only third censor," said he, "in point of age—you must first call out your own countryman, Sir Hans Sloane, our president, and when you have fought him, and two senior censors, then I shall be ready to meet you."

Many medical duels have been prevented by the difficulty of arranging the "*methodus pugnandi.*" In the instance of Dr. Brocklesby, the number of paces could not be agreed upon; and in the affair between Akenside and Ballow, one had determined never to fight in the morning, and the other that he would never fight in the afternoon.

John Wilkes, who did not stand upon ceremony in these little affairs, when asked by Lord Talbot, " How many times they were to fire ?" replied "just as often as your lordship pleases; I have brought a *bag of bullets and a flask of gunpowder with me.*"

Nothwithstanding Dr. Baillie's general amiability of character, the multiplicity of his professional concerns would often betray him into an irritability of temper. He frequently came home, after a day of great fatigue, and held up his hands to his family circle, eager to welcome him home, saying, " Don't speak to me;" and then, presently, after a glass of wine, and when the transitory cloud had cleared away from his brow, with a smile of affection, he would look round him, and exclaim: " You may speak to me now."

Dr. Sydenham still keeps his well-earned and long-acknowledged fame amidst the modern wildness of theory and singularity of practice. "*Opinionum commenta delet dies,*" says Tully very beautifully ; " *naturæ judicia confirmat.*"

Sydenham had a troop of horse when King Charles I. had made a garrison-town of Oxford, and studied medicine by accidentally falling into the company of Dr. Coxe, an eminent physician, who finding him to be a man of great parts, recommended to him his own profession, and gave him directions for his method of pursuing his studies in that art. These he pursued with such success, that in a few years afterwards he became the chief physician of the metropolis.

Sir Richard Blackmore says of him, " that he built all his maxims and rules of practice upon repeated observations on the nature and properties of disease, and on the power of remedies; and that he compiled so good a history of distempers, and so prevalent a method of cure, that he has advanced the healing art more than Dr. Wallis, with all his curious speculations and fanciful hypotheses."

In the dedication of one of his Treatises to his friend Dr. Mapletoft, Sydenham says, " that the medical art could not be learned so well and so surely as by use and experience; and that he who would pay the nicest and most accurate attention to the symptoms of distempers, would succeed best in finding out the true means of cure." He says, afterwards, " that it was no small sanction to his method, that it was approved of by Mr. Locke," of whom he adds, " whether I consider his genius, or the acuteness and accuracy of his judgment, and his ancient (that is, the best) morals, I hardly think that I can find one superior, certainly very few that are equal to him."

Sydenham had such confidence in exercise on horseback, that in one of his medical works he says, " that if any man was possessed of a remedy that would do equal service to the human constitution with riding gently on horseback twice a day, he would be in possession of the philosopher's stone."

The very extraordinary case mentioned by this great physician, of the cure of a most inveterate diarrhœa, in a learned prelate, by slow journeys on horseback, was that of Seth Ward, the Bishop of Sarum, a great mathematician, and one of the first members of the Royal

Society. It is mentioned in the life of the Bishop, by Dr. Walter Pope.

Sydenham died of the gout; and in the latter part of his life is described as visited with that dreadful disorder, and sitting near an open window, on the ground-floor of his house, in St. James's Square, respiring the cool breeze on a summer's evening, and reflecting with a serene countenance, and great complacency, on the alleviation to human misery that his skill in his art enabled him to give. Whilst this divine man was enjoying one of these delicious reveries, a thief took away from the table, near to which he was sitting, a silver tankard filled with his favourite beverage, small beer, in which a sprig of rosemary had been immersed, and ran off with it. Sydenham was too lame to ring the bell, and too feeble in his voice to give the alarm.

This great physician has been accused of discouraging students in medicine from reading works connected with their own complicated art. Sir Richard Blackmore observes, that a man of good sense, vivacity, and spirit, may arrive to the highest rank as a physician, without the assistance of great erudition and knowledge of books; and he tells us that this was the case with Dr. Sydenham, who became an eminent and an able physician, though he never designed to take up the profession until the civil wars were concluded; and then, being a disbanded officer, he entered upon it for a maintenance, without any learning properly preparatory for the undertaking of it: and to show what contempt he had for the writings in physic, when one day he asked him what books he should read to qualify him for practice, Sydenham replied, "read Don Quixote, it is a very good book, I read it still;" so low an opinion had this celebrated man of the learning collected out of the authors, his predecessors. And the late celebrated physician Dr. Radcliffe, whose judgment was universally relied upon as almost infallible in his profession, used to say, that when he died, he would leave behind him the whole mystery of physic in half a sheet of paper. "It is true," says Blackmore, "that both these doctors carried the matter much too far by vilifying learning, of which they were no masters, and perhaps for that reason."

Sir Hans Sloane, who was very well acquainted with Sydendam, says, he never knew a man of brighter natural parts than that physician, and he believes what is here said about Don Quixote, to be merely a joke; and that Tully was Dr. Sydenham's favourite author, he having a fine bust of him in his study.

Sir Hans Sloane, the celebrated physician and naturalist, was born at Killcleugh, in the South of Ireland, in 1660. He succeeded Sir Isaac Newton as president of the Royal Society, was the founder of the British Museum, and President of the College of Physicians.

He settled in London, in the year 1684, and was in high vogue as a practitioner in Radcliffe's time, with whom he was acquainted, though they were never on good terms. He continued in great practice till the year 1746, when he retired, and died fourteen years afterwards.

On his arrival in London, Sloane waited upon Sydenham, with a letter of recommendation from a friend, setting forth his qualifications in flaming terms—"he was a ripe scholar—a good botanist—a skilful anatomist, &c."

After Sydenham had perused this eulogy, and had eyed the tyro very attentively, he said: "All this is mighty fine; but it wont do! anatomy—botany—nonsense! Sir, I have an old woman in Covent Garden who understands botany better; as for anatomy my butcher can dissect a joint full as well;—no, young man, all this is stuff; you must go to the bedside, it is there you can alone learn disease."

Such was the first interview which the future President of the Royal Society, and the successor of the great Sir Isaac Newton, had with the father of English medicine, as Sydenham has been termed.

Sydenham was subsequently very kind to Sloane, and frequently took him in his chariot to Acton and back again before dinner—Sydenham's favourite ride. It was in one of these excursions that Sloane hinted his intention of going to Jamaica. Sydenham remained silent until the carriage stopped as usual at the Green Park, through which Sydenham and Sloane walked, when the doctor said: " You must not go—you had better drown yourself in Roxmond's pond, as you go along."

Sloane however went, and brought home a great variety of new plants. He was considered the greatest naturalist of his day, and his friendship and society were courted by all the literati of Europe. So passionately fond was he of botany, that he could not sleep comfortably without having in his bed-room some scarce and beautiful plant to examine before he retired to rest, and when he arose in the morning.

Sir Hans Sloane was the first English physician who was raised to the baronetage. He was a great favourite of Queen Anne's, whom he bled in her last illness. Queen Caroline also thought highly of him, and frequently consulted him. His great scientific attainments did not act as a bar to his professional advancement. His practice was very extensive.

Sir Hans Sloane bequeathed his immense library and cabinet of curiosities to the public, on condition of parliament granting to his family the sum of £20,000. The library consisted of more than fifty-thousand volumes; three hundred and forty-seven of which, were illustrated with cuts, finely engraven and coloured from nature; three thousand five hundred and sixty-six manuscripts; and an infinite number of rare and curious books. The act for the purpose of purchasing Sir H. Sloane's library and museum, was passed in 1753. The sum of £300,000 was raised by a lottery, which enabled parliament to effect their object. Besides the £20,000 paid for Sir Hans' collection, the Harleian manuscripts were purchased for £10,000, and a similar sum was given for Montague House, to which the library, manuscripts, and curiosities were removed. Thus originated the British Museum, now the resort of the most distinguished literary men and geniuses of the age: Sir Hans also gave to the Company of Apothecaries, the entire freehold of the botanical garden at Chelsea.

Although Sir Hans Sloane expended a prodigious sum of money in collecting rareties, he is said to have been of a penurious disposition. At the age of ninety he complained bitterly to Dr. Mortimer, then secretary to the Royal Society, that all his friends had deserted him; upon which the doctor observed, that Chelsea was far removed from the residence of his friends. On one occasion, when Dr. Mortimer had been detained for several hours in showing Sir Hans's famous collection to some distinguished foreigners, Sloane invited him to stop to dinner, and when it appeared, it consisted of a boiled egg, and a half-starved fowl. Upon Dr. Mortimer remonstrating with Sir Hans, he put the old baronet quite out of humour—
" Keep a table!" he exclaimed, " invite people to dinner! what! would you have me ruin myself? Public credit totters already; and if there should be a national bankruptcy, or a sponge to wipe out the national debt, you may yet see me in the work-house."

Dr. Woodward was expelled the council of the Royal Society, for an insult offered to Sir Hans, then Dr. Sloane the secretary. Sir Hans was reading a paper of his own composition, and Woodward said something greatly insulting about it. Sir Isaac Newton was in the chair when the vote for expulsion was agitated. Dr. Sloane complained that he had often affronted him by making grimaces at him; and upon that occasion Dr. Arbuthnot got up to ask what degree of distortion of the muscles of a man's face it was that constituted a grimace? Woodward, however, was expelled; and some body having pleaded in his favour that he was a good natural philosopher, Sir Isaac Newton remarked, that in order to belong to that society, a man ought to be a good *moral philosopher, as well as a natural one.*

Woodward was an eccentric, turbulent, and vain man. Bromfield's father, who was a commissioner of the stamp office, used often to meet Woodward at Rando's coffee-house. Woodward was one day wondering how the great lived so long as they did, considering their luxurious mode of living—"to day," says he for instance, " I dined with the archbishop of Canterbury, and the venison was so rich, that I feel myself much disordered by it." A wag who overheard the conversation, and who had seen the doctor that day at dinner at a chop-house, cried out, " you and I, doctor, ate off the same haunch; only a very thin partition parted us."

Dr. W. Woodville flourished in the year 1791. He wrote a celebrated work on botany, and was physician to the small-pox hospital. He was engaged in a controversy with Dr. Jenner respecting the efficacy of the vaccine virus. The characteristics of his genius were judgment, caution, and prudence. He has been accused of intemperate habits; but this has been most positively denied.

Medical men are said to meet their end with composure. When Dr. Woodville was supposed to be dangerously ill, his friends called upon him and endeavoured to excite his hopes of recovery: " I am not so silly," said the doctor, " as to mind what they say; I know my own case too well, and that I am dying: a younger person with a better stamina, might think it hard to die, but why should I regret to leave such a diseased worn-out carcass as mine?" The carpenter with whom he lodged, had not been always on the best terms with Woodville. The physician said he should wish to let the man see that he died in peace with him; and as he had never much occasion to employ him, desired he might be sent for to measure him for his coffin. This was accordingly done; the carpenter came, and took the measure of the doctor, who begged him not to be more than two days about it, "for," said he, "I shall not live beyond that time;" and he did actually die just before the end of the next day. He got between one or two thousand pounds by his "Medical Botany," and with the money bought a small estate, which he left to his natural daughter, being all the property he possessed.

Dr. WILLIAM HUNTER was one of the most distinguished scientific physicians of his day. He was originally destined for the church, but having formed the friendship of the illustrious Dr. Cullen, he resolved to embrace the profession of physic. A conversation took place one evening after Dr. Cullen had finished his arduous labours of the day, relating to the respective positions of the members of the medical and clerical profession, Hunter taking one side, and Dr. Cullen the other. The question was, which produced the greater amount of mental pleasure. During the conversation, a message came for Cullen to attend immediately a patient represented to be dangerously ill. "Come with me, Hunter," said the doctor, "and I will introduce you to the sick chamber." Conjointly they visited the sick man's habitation. Cullen found his patient labouring under a serious attack of *gastritis*, attended with excruciating agony. The friends of the invalid were in the greatest apprehension that if relief was not instantly administered, death would ensue. Cullen directly ordered copious general and local bleeding, with medicines which he thought necessary. The patient was bled, and Cullen and Hunter waited anxiously to witness the result. A mitigation of the urgent symptoms was the effect of the remedies had recourse to, and expressions of deep and lasting gratitude were showered down upon the physician's head. This appeared to make a due impression on Hunter's mind, and he exclaimed to Cullen, as they were going home, " Yours is indeed a noble science, and I will devote my existence in attempting to enlarge its boundaries." Thus commenced this great man's

career. In after life he distinguished himself as an
anatomist, physiologist, a lecturer, and an accoucheur.
The splendid museum attached to the University of
Glasgow, is a lasting monument to his fame. He was a
fellow of the Royal Society, President of the Medical
Society, and Accoucheur to the Middlesex Hospital, and
British Lying-in Hospital. He had the honour of attending the Queen in her *accouchement*, and he was of course
appointed Physician Extraordinary to her Majesty. He
contributed several valuable additions to medical literature, particularly in reference to the branch of science
which he practised. A short period before he died, he
rose from his bed to deliver an introductory lecture on the
Operations of Surgery, in opposition to the earnest re-
monstrances of his friends. The lecture was accordingly
delivered, but it was his last. Towards the conclusion,
his strength was so much exhausted that he fainted away,
and was finally replaced in his chamber, which he had
been so eager to quit. Turning to his friend Combe, in
his latter moments, he observed, " If I had strength
enough to hold a pen, I would write how easy and
pleasant a thing it is to die." His death took place on
the 30th of March, 1783.

We must not omit, in our enumeration of Medical
Philanthropists, the name of HAWES, the founder of that
excellent institution, the *Humane Society.*

Dr. Hawes was born at Islington, and received his
classical education at St. Paul's school. In 1773 he became very popular, owing to his incessant zeal in calling
the attention of the public to the resuscitation of persons
apparently dead, principally by drowning. In this laudable attempt he encountered much opposition and ridicule.
The practicability of resuscitation was denied. He ascertained, however, its feasibility. He advertised rewards to
person who should, within a certain time after any accident, between Westminster and London Bridges, rescue
apparently drowned persons from the water, and bring

them ashore to places appointed for their reception, where means might be used for their recovery, on their giving immediate notice to him. The public mind being thus awakened to the subject, greater exertions were made by individuals than had ever been before known; and many lives were saved by himself and other medical men. Mr. Hawes, at his own expense, paid the rewards in these cases for twelve months, which amounted to a considerable sum. His excellent friend, Dr. Cogan, who had long turned his attention to this subject, remonstrated with him on the injury which his private fortune would sustain from a perseverance in these expenses, and he at last consented to share them with the public. Dr. Cogan and he agreed to join their strength, and each of them bringing forward fifteen friends to a meeting at the Chapter Coffee-house, in 1774, the Humane Society was instantly formed.

The late Dr. GLOVER, of convivial memory, though regularly bred to physic and surgery, was for a short period in his early life an actor on the Dublin stage, during which time he conceived the idea that many persons, in a state of suspended animation, might, by proper and timely treatment, be restored to society. The doctor was so confident of his opinion being well-founded, that he laid a wager with a brother comedian, that the first malefactor who was executed he would restore to life. The bet was accepted, and a few days after the doctor had an opportunity of proving that he was right, on the apparently dead body of a man who was hanged for a robbery. He was, however, rather unfortunate in the choice of his subject; for the following day the fellow having discovered the doctor's lodgings, and being introduced into the apartment where he was sitting, the resuscitated criminal, accosting the preserver of his life by the familiar appellation of " *Father*," said, that as he had restored him to existence, it was his duty to support him as his son, and this he should expect him to do. The singularity of the application so amazed the doctor, that it was some time before he recovered his powers sufficiently to enable him to expel him *vi et armis* from the room. Nothing daunted by his reception, he visited the theatre that evening, and harangued the audience from the gallery, whilst the doctor was acting. Wherever the poor doctor went, his resuscitated friend followed him, demanding a settlement for life. At last Dr. Glover was compelled, in order to get rid of his *hopeful heir*, to offer to advance him a sum of money if he would leave the kingdom. This was accordingly agreed to.

DR. GEORGE FORDYCE was one of the most eminent and successful lecturers of his day. He was the friend and companion of Dr. Cullen, whom he turned " his learned and revered master." He was much censured for his intemperate habits. He frequently has been known to have been up all night, and to have lectured to his class for three hours the next morning, without having undressed himself. He had a most retentive memory.

He read but little, but what he did read he remembered. His appearance was by no means prepossessing. His countenance was dull and heavy, and not at all indicative of his mind.

This celebrated lecturer dined every day for more than twenty years at Dolly's chop-house. His researches in comparative anatomy had led him to conclude, that man, through custom, eats oftener than nature requires, one meal a day being sufficient for that noble animal the lion. At four o'clock, his accustomed hour of dining, the doctor regularly took the seat at the table always reserved for him, on which was placed a silver tankard full of strong ale, a bottle of port wine, and a •measure containing a quarter of a pint of brandy. The moment the waiter announced him, the cook put a pound and a half of rump steak on the gridiron, and on the table some delicate trifle, as a *bonne bouche*, to serve until the steak was ready. This, was sometimes half a boiled chicken, sometimes a plate of fish : when he had eaten this, he took one glass of brandy, and then proceeded to devour his steak. When he had finished his meal, he took the remainder of his brandy, having during his dinner drank the tankard of ale, and afterwards a bottle of port ! He thus daily spent an hour and a half of his time, and then returned to his house in Essex Street, to give his six o'clock lecture on chemistry. He made no other meal until his return, at four o'clock next day, to Dolly's.

When Fordyce was near his latter end, he desired his youngest daughter, who was sitting by his bedside, to take up a book and read to him ; she read for about twenty minutes, when the doctor said, " stop, go out of the room, I am going to die." She put down the book, and left the chamber to call an attendant, who immediately went into the bed-room, and found Fordyce had breathed his last.

DR. GEORGE CHEYNE, the author of the celebrated work, entitled "The English Malady," graduated at Edinburgh. He was originally intended for the Church, but abandoned the study of theology for medicine, after having heard Dr. Pitcairn's lectures. In his autobiography he says : " when coming up to London, I all of a sudden, changed my whole manner of living. I found the bottle companions, the younger gentry, and free livers, to be the most easy of access, or most quickly susceptible of friendship and acquaintance; nothing being necessary for that purpose but to eat lustily, and to swallow down much liquor." The doctor, found, however, that his health became seriously affected, and he accordingly resolved to change his mode of living. He adopted a milk and vegetable diet, and recovered his strength, activity, and cheerfulness.

He died at Bath, in 1743, where he had been for a long period, in rather extensive practice. Among his patients, was the celebrated Beau Nash ; who on being asked one day, by Cheyne, if he had followed his last prescription, replied in the negative; adding, "If I had, doctor, I should certainly have broken my neck, for I threw it out of a two pair of stairs' window."

A lady, whose fondness for generous living, had given her a flushed face and carbuncled nose, consulted Dr. Cheyne. Upon surveying herself in the glass she exclaimed, "Where in the name of wonder, doctor, did I get such a nose as this?" "Out of the decanter, Madam, out of the decanter," replied the doctor.

A patient, accompanied by Beau Nash visited Dr. Cheyne, for the purpose of ascertaining the cause of a slight abdominal swelling, under which he was labouring. On examining the patient, the doctor pronounced the swelling to be occasioned by a collection of water, and that it would be necessary to be tapped. "It cannot be water," said the patient, "it may be wine." "No, no, my good fellow," said Nash, "if it had been wine, you would long before this have tapped it yourself."

Dr. Cheyne always enforced the doctrines he taught by his personal example. This conduct created him a host of enemies, who attacked, but never defeated, their intrepid antagonist; and the following *jeu d'esprit*, though often related, proves the assertion.

DR. WINTER TO DR. CHEYNE, BATH.

"Tell me whence, fat-headed Scot,
    Thy system thou didst learn?
From Hippocrates thou hadst it not,
    Nor Celsus, nor Pitcairn.

"What, though we own that milk is good,*
    And say the same of grass,
The one—for babes is proper food,
    The other for an ass.

---

* Dr. Cheyne wrote a treatise, in which he recommends to invalids a milk diet.

"Doctor, a new prescription try—
  A friend's advice forgive;
Eat grass—reduce your head—or die,
  Your patients then may live."

DR. CHEYNE'S REPLY.

"My system, doctor, 's all my own,
  No tutor I pretend;
My blunders hurt myself alone,
  But yours—your dearest friend.

"Were you once more to straw confined,
  How happy it might be—
You would, perhaps, regain your mind,
  Or from your *wit* get free.

"I can't your new prescription try,
  But easily forgive;
'Tis nat'ral you should bid me die,
  That you yourself may live."

Dr. Cheyne and Tadlow were exceedingly corpulent men, but the last was much the larger. Cheyne coming into a coffee-house one morning, and observing Tadlow alone and pensive, asked him what occasioned his melancholy. "Cheyne," said he, "I have a very serious thought come athwart me; I am considering how the people will be able to get you and me to the grave when we die." "Why," said Cheyne, "six or eight strong fellows may take me there at once; but it is certain that *you* must be carried there *twice*."

In Dr. Cheyne's "English Malady," we find the extraordinary case of Colonel Townshend related, which being singular we shall insert in the doctor's own words. "Colonel Townshend, a gentleman of excellent natural parts, and of great honour and integrity, had for many years been afflicted with a nephritic complaint which made his life miserable. During one of his attacks of illness he sent for Dr. Baynard and myself: we waited upon him with Mr. Skrine, his apothecary. We found his senses clear and mind calm: his nurse and several servants were about him. He had made his will and settled his affairs. He told us he had sent for us to give some account of an odd sensation he had for some time observed and felt within himself; which was, that composing himself he could die or expire whenever he pleased, *by an effort of the will*, and, by another effort, could come to life again, which it seems he had sometimes tried before he had sent for us: we heard this with surprise, but as it was to be accounted for on no common principles, we could hardly believe the facts he related to us, much less give any account of it, unless he should please to make the experiment before us, which we were unwilling he should do, lest, in his weak condition, he might carry it too far. He continued to talk very distinctly and sensibly for above a quarter of an hour, about this surprising sensation, and insisted so much on our seeing the trial made, that we were at last forced to comply. We all three felt his pulse first, it was distinct, although small and steady; and his heart had its usual beating. He composed himself on his back, and lay in a still posture for some time: while I held his right hand, Dr. Baynard laid his hand on his heart, and Mr. Skrine held a clean looking-glass to his mouth. I found his pulse sink gradually, until at last I could not feel any, by the most exact and nice touch; Dr. Baynard could not feel the least motion in his heart, nor Mr. Skrine perceive the least soil of breath on the bright mirror he held to his mouth: then each of us by turns examined his arm, heart, and breath, but could not by the nicest scrutiny discover the least symptom of life in him. We reasoned a long time about his odd appearance as well as we could, and all of us judging it inexplicable and unaccountable, and finding he still continued in that condition, we began to conclude that he had indeed carried the experiment too far, and at last were satisfied he was actually dead, and were just ready to leave him. This continued for half an hour. As we were leaving, we observed some motion about the body; and, upon examination, we found his pulse and the motion of the heart gradually returning: he began to breathe gently and to speak softly, and after some conversation with him we left him. He afterwards sent for his attorney, added a codicil to his will, settled legacies on his servants, received the sacrament, and calmly and composedly expired, about five or six o'clock that evening."

DR. WILLIAM HARVEY conferred upon the science of medicine, by his discovery of the circulation of the blood, the same service which the immortal Newton rendered to optics and astronomy, by his theories of light and gravitation.

Harvey was educated at a grammar school in Canterbury, and subsequently he entered Cambridge University. In 1602 he took his degree of M. D. at Padua, when he was only twenty-four years of age. Harvey was engaged twenty-six years in prosecuting his inquiries into the circulation of the blood, and in bringing his great work to maturity. When his discovery was made known, he was treated by his adversaries with contempt and reproach. To an intimate friend he confessed, that after his book of the circulation came out, he fell considerably in his practice, and it was believed by the vulgar that he was crack-brained: all his contemporary physicians were against his opinions, and envied him the fame he was likely to acquire by his discovery. That reputation, he did, however, ultimately enjoy: about twenty-five years after the publication of his system, it was received in all the Universities of the world: and Hobbes has observed, that "Harvey was the only man, perhaps, who ever lived to see his own doctrines established in his lifetime."

The original MSS. of Harvey's lectures are preserved

in the British Museum; and some very curious preparations, which either he himself made at Padua, or procured
from that celebrated school of medicine, and which most
probably he exhibited to his class, during his course of
lectures on the circulation, are now in the College of
Physicians; they consist of six tables or boards, upon
which are spread the different nerves or blood-vessels,
carefully dissected out of the body: in one of them the
semilunar valves of the aorta are distinctly to be seen.
Now these valves, placed at the origin of the arteries,
must, together with the valves of the veins, have furnished
Harvey with the most striking and conclusive arguments
in support of his novel doctrines.

During Harvey's stay at Oxford he became acquainted
with a young physician, Dr. Charles Scarborough, who
was afterwards knighted by Charles II. Harvey delighted
much in the conversation of Scarborough, who was, however, in those troublesome times, much disposed to neglect
his medical studies for the more brilliant profession of
arms. To check this military ardour, Harvey took the
young doctor, and accommodated him with a lodging in
his own apartment, saying, "Prithee, leave off thy gun-
ning, and stay here; I will bring thee into practice."

" When I was at Padua in 1787," says Dr. Moseley " I
looked for the arms of the great Harvey, among a multitude which adorn the public hall of the University; but
his were not there. There were several of the English,
of his standing. It was the custom at Padua, for every
person who had taken a doctor's degree to have his arms
and name hung up in the University, when he went away.

" After such a lapse of time, it was not likely that I
should obtain any anecdotes concerning him at Padua;
but I did not omit to inquire. Among other things, on
which I could obtain no additional information, was the
tradition of the extraordinary preservation of his life, in
the commencement of his journey to Padua; in which
there appeared an interposition of something more than
human intelligence.

"When Harvey arrived at Dover, with several other young men, in order to embark for the continent, in their way to Italy, they went with their passports to Sir Henry Brooke, then commanding at Dover Castle. When Harvey presented his passport, Sir Henry told him he should not go; but must remain his prisoner. Harvey desired to know the reason, and to be informed what offence he had committed. The Governor replied it was his pleasure; and gave him no further satisfaction. In the evening, which was beautifully clear, the packet sailed with Harvey's companions on board. In the night there arose a terrible storm, in which the vessel was lost, and all on board perished.

"The next day the melancholy news was brought to Dover. The Governor then explained himself to Harvey, whom he knew only by sight. He told him that, on the night before his arrival, he had a perfect vision of him in a dream, coming to Dover to cross over to Calais; and that he had a warning to stop him. Great and glorious, indeed, was the use which Harvey made of a life so miraculously protected!

Harvey was a great martyr to the gout, and his method of treating himself was as follows:—"He would sit with his legs bare, even if it were frosty, on the leads of Cochaine House, where he lived for some time with his brother Eliab, or put them into a pail of water until he was almost dead with cold; and then he would betake himself to his stove. He was troubled with insomnolency, to cure which he would rise in the night, and walk about his chamber in his shirt until he began to shiver, and then he would return to his bed."

Harvey died worth £20,000.

Dr. JOHN FRIEND, the author of the "History of Medicine," which was written during his confinement in the Tower, was born in 1675. After his liberation he was appointed physician to the Prince of Wales; on whose accession to the throne he became physician to the Queen.

Friend, who was generally what is termed mellow after dinner, was once sent for in this state, to a family of consequence; but the family not choosing to trust to his prescription, sent for Dr. Mead, who came, and, after looking at what Friend had written, took the opportunity of paying him a very high compliment. " 'Pon my word," said Mead, " if Dr. Friend wrote this when he was drunk, he prescribes better than I can do when sober."

It should be recollected that intemperance was the common vice of the age; and physicians not being exempted from the frailties of the flesh, occasionally indulged in " potations pottle deep."

Dr. Beauford, a Jacobite physician, was much addicted to this vice. He was a man, however, of great eminence, and intimate with Lord Barrymore, who was thought to favour the Pretender, in 1745, and Beauford was taken up and examined by the privy-council. He was asked if he knew Lord Barrymore ? " Yes."—" You are often with him?" " Very often dine with him."— " And what do you talk about ?" " Eating and drinking; nothing but eating and drinking." And this was all they could get out of him : so he was dismissed.

The same Dr. Beauford, used to dine every week, on a particular day, at a tavern in Finch Lane. Apothecaries used to come and consult him, but no one was ever allowed to drink out of his bottle. Many whimsical anecdotes are recorded of this physician, who was desirous of passing himself off for a wit.—" Why do you not admire my daughter ?" said a lady to the doctor, " Because," said he, " I am no judge of *painting*." " But, surely," rejoined the lady, not the least disconcerted by this rude reflection, " you never saw an angel that was *not* painted !"

The following anecdote of the illness of Bishop Newton, whom Dr. Friend attended, may prove interesting :—

He says, in his autobiography, that he was seized with

a violent pleuritic fever—his illness cost him seven hundred and fifty guineas for physicians, and his cure was at last effected by *small beer*. Dr. Hope, Dr. Swynsen, and other physicians from Stafford, Lichfield, and Derby, were called in, and had two hundred and fifty guineas of the money. Dr. Friend came down post from London, with Mrs. Pulteney, and received three hundred guineas for his journey. Dr. Broxholme came from Oxford, and received two hundred guineas. When these physicians, who were his particular friends, arrived, they found the case quite desperate, and gave him entirely over. They said every thing had been done that could be done. They prescribed some few medicines, but without the least effect. He was still alive, and was heard to mutter, in a low voice, "Small beer, Small beer!" They said, give him small beer, or any thing. Accordingly a great silver cup was brought, which contained two quarts of small beer. They ordered an orange to be squeezed into it, and gave it to him. He drank the whole at a draught, and called for another. Another was given him, and, soon after drinking that, he fell into a most profound sleep, and a most profuse sweat for nearly twenty-two hours. In him the saying was verified, " *If he sleep he shall do well.*" From that time he recovered marvellously, insomuch that, in a few days, the physicians took their leave, saying that, " Now he had no want of any thing but a horse for his doctor, and an ass for his apothecary."

Friend died in the year 1728. The following lines are from the pen of Samuel Wesley :—

" When Radcliffe fell, afflicted Physic cried,
  ' How vain my powers !' and languished at his side.
  When Friend expired, deep struck, her hair she tore,
  And, speechless, fainted, and reviv'd no more.
  Her flowing grief no further could extend ;
  She mourns with Radcliffe, but she dies with Friend."

Dr. JOHN ARBUTHNOT was Queen Anne's favourite physician, the friend of Swift and Pope. It is said that he
possessed all the wit of the Dean, without any of his
virulence and indelicacy; and a considerable portion of
the genius of Pope, without his querulous discontent.
When a young man he attempted to settle as a physician,
at Dorchester, a town remarkable for its healthy situation, a circumstance unpropitious to the profitable practice of physic. On quitting it, a friend met him riding
post to London. " Where are you going, Arbuthnot?"
asked his friend. " To leave your confounded place, for
a man can neither live nor die there," replied Arbuthnot.

Arbuthnot affords a striking instance how little misfortune can derange or exhaust the internal resources of a
good man; for, " I am as well," said he, in a letter written a few weeks before he died, " as a man can be, who
is gasping for breath, and has a house full of men and
women unprovided for." Every branch of his family,
however, passed through life with competence and honour.

The great have always been flattered, but never was
adulation carried farther than on the part of Dr. Arbuthnot to Queen Anne. The Queen, having asked him
what the time was, he replied, bowing with much grace,
" Whatever it may please your Majesty."

Arbuthnot was distinguished as a wit, and as a successful dramatic writer. During his time, Gulliver's
Travels made their appearance, and he relates several
amusing instances of the effect which this celebrated
piece of satire had on the public mind.

Dr. Arbuthnot says, that Lord Scarborough (who was
no inventor of stories) told him, that he happened to be
in company with a master of a ship, who said, that " he
was very well acquainted with Mr. Gulliver: but that the
printer had made a mistake, for it was at *Wapping*, and
not at Rotherhithe, that the Captain lived."

In another place, Dr. Arbuthnot says: " I lent Gulliver's Travels to an old gentleman to read; who, putting on his spectacles, went very deliberately to his map to look for " *Lilliput.*"

Mr. Fortescue (afterwards Master of the Rolls,) when a lawyer on the Western Circuit, wrote a letter to Mr. Pope, in the year 1727, stating that " One Lemuel Gulliver had a cause there, and lost it on the ill-reputation he had acquired of being a most notorious liar:" and an Irish judge told some person of Swift's acquaintance, very gravely, that he looked upon the whole of Gulliver's Travels, (*whatever other persons might think of them,*) to be one continued heap of improbable lies.

We should be guilty of a great dereliction of duty were we to omit to give a sketch of the life of Dr. ED-WARD JENNER, the immortal discoverer of vaccination. The name of this physician certainly deserves a place among the great and illustrious benefactors of the human race. The history of Jenner, it is observed, exhibits the life-long efforts of a man of philosophical character and constant habits of observation, catching a glimpse, early in his professional life, of a truth of the highest pathological importance, connected with a discovery of amazing benefit to mankind; we see him keeping this object in view, clearing away the obstacles between him and it, regarding the question on every side, and submitting it with equal industry, candour, and simplicity of mind, to the inspection of every eye; and labouring incessantly for its establishment when fully convinced of its real and incalculable value, despite of cold disregard and vehement opposition, misrepresentation, calumny, and ridicule; but sometimes with the cheering sympathy of noble minds and the approving judgment of some of the first men of his time.

The first intimation received by Jenner of the possible existence of a disease communicated by contact with the cow, and capable of protecting the affected individual from the occurrence of small-pox, was given to him when he was an apprentice with a surgeon at Sodbury.

He was pursuing his professional education in the house of his master, when a young woman came to seek advice; the subject of small-pox was mentioned in her presence; she immediately observed, "I cannot take that disease, for I have had cow-pox." This incident rivetted the attention of Jenner, and made an impression on his mind which was never effaced.

Sir Isaac Newton, unfolded his doctrine of light and colours before he was twenty; Bacon wrote his "*Temporis Partus Maximus*" before he attained that age; Montesquieu had sketched his "Spirit of Laws," at an equally early period of life; and Jenner, when he was still younger, contemplated the possibility of removing from among the list of human diseases one of the most mortal that ever scourged our race.

As far back as the year 1775, Dr. Jenner had begun to investigate the nature of the cow-pox. His attention to this singular disease was first excited, in addition to the circumstance just related, by observing, that among those whom in the country he was frequently called upon to inoculate, many resisted every effort to give them the small-pox. These patients he found had undergone a disorder contracted by milking cows affected with a peculiar eruption on their teats. On inquiry, it appeared that this disease had been known among the dairies from time immemorial, and that a vague opinion prevailed of its being a preventive of the small-pox. This opinion, however, was comparatively new, for all the old farmers declared they had no such idea in early days, which was easily accounted for, as the common people were rarely inoculated for the small-pox, till the practice became extended by the improved method of the Suttons; so that the people in the dairies were seldom put to the test of the preventive powers of the cow-pox.

In the course of *his* investigations, Dr. Jenner found

that some of those who seemed to have undergone the cow-pox, on inoculation with variolous matter, felt its influence just the same as if no disease had been communicated from the cow. On making inquiries on the subject among the medical practitioners in his neighbourhood, they all agreed that the cow-pox was not to be relied upon as a preventive of the small-pox. This for a while damped, but did not extinguish his ardour; for, as he proceeded, he had the satisfaction of learning that the cow was subject to some varieties of spontaneous eruptions upon her teats; that they were all capable of communicating sores to the hands of the milkers; and that whatever sore was derived from the animal obtained the general name of the cow-pox. Thus a great obstacle was surmounted, and in consequence a distinction was discovered between the true and the spurious cow-pox.

But the first impediment to this inquiry had not been long removed before another, of greater magnitude, started up. There were not wanting instances to prove, that when the true cow-pox broke out among the cattle, a person who had milked the infected animal, and had thereby apparently gone through the disease in common with others, was yet liable to receive the small-pox. This gave a painful check to the fond and aspiring hopes of Jenner; till, reflecting that the operations of nature are generally uniform, and that it was not probable the human constitution, after undergoing the cow-pox, should in some instances be perfectly shielded from the small-pox, and in others remain unprotected, he determined to renew his laborious investigation of the subject. The result was fortunate : for he now discerned that the virus of the cow-pox was liable to undergo progressive changes, from the same causes precisely as that of small-pox; and that when applied to the human skin in a degenerated state, it would produce the ulcerative effects in as great a degree as when it was not decomposed, and even sometimes greater; but that when its specific properties were lost, it was incapable of producing that change upon the human frame which is requisite to render it unsusceptible of the variolous contagion: so that it became evident a person might milk a cow one day, and having caught the disease, be for ever secure; while on another person, milking the same cow the next day, the virus might act in such a way as to produce sores, and yet leave the constitution unchanged, and therefore unprotected.

During this investigation of the casual cow-pox, as received by contact with the animal, our inquirer was struck with the idea that it might be practicable to propagate the disease by inoculation, after the manner of the small-pox, first from the cow, and finally from one human being to another. He waited anxiously some time for an opportunity of putting this theory to the test. At length the period of trial arrived; and on the 14th of May, 1796, the first experiment was made upon a lad of the name of Phipps, in whose arm a little vaccine virus was inserted, taken from the hand of a young woman, of the name of Sarah Nelmes, who had been accidentally infected by a cow. Notwithstanding the resemblance which the pustule, thus excited in the boy's arm, bore to variolous inoculation, yet as the indisposition attending it was barely perceptible, the operator could scarcely persuade himself that his patient was secure from the small-pox. However, on the same boy being inoculated on the 1st of July following with small-pox matter, it proved that he was perfectly safe. This case inspired confidence; and, as soon as a supply of proper virus could be obtained from the cow, arrangements were made for a series of inoculations. A number of children were inoculated in succession, one from the other; and after several months had elapsed, they were exposed to the infection of the small-pox, some by inoculation, others by variolous effluvia, and some in both ways; but they all resisted it. The result of these trials gradually led to a wider field of experiment; and when at length it was satisfactorily proved that the inoculated cow-pox afforded as complete a security against the small-pox as the variolous inoculation, the author of the discovery made it known to the public, without either disguise or ostentation. This treatise, entitled "An Inquiry into the Causes and Effects of the Variolæ Vaccinæ, a disease discovered in some of the Western Counties of England, particularly Gloucestershire, and known by the name of the Cow-pox," appeared in 1798, in a small quarto of seventy-five pages.

It was not until the year 1780, that Dr. Jenner communicated to his friend, Edward Gardner, his hopes and fears respecting the great object of his pursuit. He was riding with this gentleman, on the road between Gloucester and Bristol, near Newport, when the conversation alluded to took place. Jenner went over the natural history of cow-pox; stated his opinion as to the origin of this affection from the heel of the horse; specified the different sorts of disease which attacked the milkers when they handled infected cows; dwelt upon that variety which afforded protection against the small-pox; and with deep and anxious emotion, mentioned his hope of being able to propagate that variety from one human being to another, till he had disseminated the practice all over the globe, to the total extinction of small-pox. The conversation was concluded by Jenner in words to the following effect: "Gardiner, I have intrusted a most important matter to you, which I firmly believe will prove of essential benefit to the human race. I know you, and should not wish what I have stated, to be brought into conversation; for should any thing untoward turn up in my experiments, I should be made, particularly by my medical brethren, the subject of ridicule—for I am the mark they all shoot at."

Dr. Jenner, in promulgating his great discovery, had many difficulties to encounter, and prejudices to remove. He was not, however, easily discouraged. In spite of all opposition, which at one time assumed a formidable character, he clearly established the truth of his principles, and induced the profession and the public to pay him that homage which he was so justly entitled to expect. So highly did the legislature think of the value of Jenner's discovery, that in July, 1807, Parliament voted him the sum of £20,000. The practice of vaccination was not confined to medical men, for many clergymen were in the habit of performing the operation. Rowland Hill, the late eminent preacher, ably defended Dr. Jenner's discovery against its opponents. "This," he said, "is the very thing for me;" and wherever he went to preach, he announced after his sermon, "I am ready to vaccinate to-morrow morning, as many children as you choose; and if you wish them to escape that horrid disease, the small-pox, you will bring them." Once a week he inoculated the children who were brought to him from Wotton and the neighbourhood; and it is well known that one of the most effective vaccine boards in London, was established, and still continues in operation, at Surrey Chapel. Mr. Hill once introduced Jenner to a nobleman, in these terms: "Allow me to present to your lordship my friend, Dr. Jenner, who has been the means of saving more lives than any other man." "Ah!" said Jenner, "would I, like you, could say *souls*."*

Dr. Baron says, that in a visit which he paid to Jenner, he showed him the hide of the cow that afforded the matter which infected Sarah Nelmes, and from which source he derived the virus that produced the disease in his first patient, Phipps. The hide hung in the coach-house: he said, "What shall I do with it?" I replied (says Dr. Baron), "Send it to the British Museum." The cow had been turned out to end her days peaceably at Broadstone, a farm near Berkeley.

Dr. Jenner often alluded to the effects of his discovery on some of his sapient townsfolk. One lady, of no mean

---

* Sidney's Life of R. Hill.

influence among them, met him soon after the publication of his Inquiry. She accosted him in this form, and in true Gloucestershire dialect. "So your book is out at last. Well! I can tell you that there be'ant a copy sold in our town; nor sha'nt, neither, if I can help it." On another occasion, the same notable dame having heard some rumours of failures in vaccination, came to the doctor with great eagerness, and said, "Shan't us have a general inoculation now?" These anecdotes Jenner related in perfect good humour.

The celebrated Charles Fox, during a residence at Cheltenham, had frequent intercourse with Jenner. His mind had been a good deal poisoned as to the character of cow-pox by his family-physician, Moseley. In his usual playful and engaging manner, he said one day to Jenner: "Pray, Dr. Jenner, tell me of this cow-pox that we have heard so much about;—what is it like?" "Why, it is exactly like the section of a pearl on a rose-leaf." This comparison, which is not less remarkable for its accuracy than for its poetic beauty, struck Mr. Fox very forcibly.

In the drawing-room of St. James's he chanced to overhear a noble lord, who was high in office, mentioning his name, and repeating the idle calumny which had been propagated concerning his own want of confidence in vaccination. He with great promptitude and decision, refuted the charge and abashed the reporter. His person was not known to the noble lord, but with entire composure he advanced to his lordship, and looking fully in his face, calmly observed, "I am Dr. Jenner." The effect of this well-timed rebuke was instantaneous. The noble lord, though "made of sterner stuff" than most men, immediately retired, and left Jenner in possession of the field.

The great opponent of vaccination was Dr. Moseley, physician to the Chelsea Hospital and to the prime minister. The doctor saw, in distinct prospect, an awful aggravation of human ills from the admixture of humours with the " cow-mania," as he termed it.   Cases were published in which vaccinated persons became covered with hair, and even exhibited horns and a tail; and that of a child was cited, whose natural disposition was so brutified that it ran on all fours, bellowing like a bull. Jenner was ridiculed in various publications; squibs and satires were resorted to in order to prejudice the public mind against vaccination. He was caricatured riding on a cow.

The following lines appeared on the subject.

" Oh, Moseley ! thy book nightly phantasies rousing,
  Full oft makes me quake for my heart's dearest treasure;
  For fancy, in dreams, oft presents them all browsing
  On commons, just like little Nebuchadnezzar.
  There, nibbling at thistle, stand Jim, Joe, and Mary,
  On their foreheads, O horrible ! crumpled horns bud;
  There Tom with his tail, and poor William all hairy,
  Reclined in a corner, are chewing the cud."

In the early part of Jenner's career he is said to have amused himself by extemporaneous versification, chiefly facetious and epigrammatic; of which the following specimen, which a lady received from him with a couple of ducks, has been preserved:

" I've despatched, my dear madam, this scrap of a letter,
  To say that Miss ——— is very much better;
  A regular doctor no longer she lacks,
  And, therefore, I've sent her a couple of quacks."

The last words which this eminent philanthropist uttered, were to the following effect: " I do not marvel that men are grateful to me; but I am surprised that they do not feel gratitude to God for making me a medium of good."

Dr. Jenner died suddenly of apoplexy, on the 26th of January, 1823. The following lines are engraven on his monument:

" Within this tomb hath found a resting-place,
The great physician of the human race—
Immortal Jenner! whose gigantic mind
Brought life and health to more than half mankind.
Let rescued infancy his worth proclaim,
And lisp out blessings on his honoured name!
And radiant beauty drop her saddest tear,
For beauty's truest, trustiest friend lies here."

The illustrious DR. JAMES GREGORY succeeded Cullen in the chair of the Practice of Medicine, at the University of Edinburgh, in the year 1776, at the early age of twenty-three. For above thirty years he annually taught the medical students the most important part of their professional duties; and an admiration of his abilities, and reverence for his character, extended as far as the English language was spoken, and as far as the light of civilization had spread in the world. His celebrated work *Conspectus Medicinæ Theoreticæ* remains to this day a standard authority with medical men.

Great, however, as was his reputation as a professor, as a man of science and literature, it was yet inferior to that which his character had acquired among his own personal friends. Descended by the father's side from a long and memorable line of ancestors, among whom the friend and contemporary of Newton is remembered—and by the mother's, from one of the most ancient noble families of Scotland—his character was early formed on an elevated model; and throughout his whole life he combined, in a degree seldom equalled, the studies and acquirements of a man of science, with the taste and honourable feeling of a high-born gentleman. His society was sought after by the first persons of rank and eminence in this country. The brilliancy of his wit, and the epigrammatic force of his conversation was long remembered by those who had the good fortune to enjoy his acquaintance. To the poorer classes his advice was at all times afforded gratuitously.

Among the many amusing illustrations with which Dr. Gregory enlivened his lectures, he used to relate the following remarkable case of.loss of memory. He wrote to a gentleman in the country, with whom he was acquainted, to come to Edinburgh to attend the funeral of a mutual friend. The gentleman obeyed the summons; but when he arrived at the doctor's house, he had totally forgotten the object of his visit. A few hours afterwards, hearing some one mention the doctor's name, he said he was very glad to hear that the doctor was in Edinburgh, forgetting that he had just parted from him. When in London, he forgot the place where his lodgings were, and it was with great difficulty that he again reached his home. After this, he always carried about with him, fastened to his coat, a piece of paper with his name and place of abode written upon it.—Another anecdote which the doctor used to relate, may serve as a caution to his less-experienced brethren. A gentleman, whose temper had been irritated by some occurrence that had taken place in his family, locked himself up in his dining-room. After waiting several hours, the family became alarmed, and bursting open the door, discovered the unfortunate gentleman lying on the floor insensible. A physician was sent for, who immediately directed the patient's head to be shaved, and applied a large blister. Mustard sina. pisms were placed on his feet, and he was bled. The young doctor prognosticating a favourable issue, took his leave, promising to see his patient early in the morning. On his arrival, to his infinite surprise, he found his patient in full health, but bitterly complaining of blisters, bleedings, and sinapisms. The secret was now explained. The poor gentleman had sought for consolation in the wine-bottle, and had, unthinkingly, drank such a quantity as to throw him into this pseudo-apoplexy.

Dr. Gregory enjoyed a large share of private practice, and was most highly esteemed by all who had occasion to consult him. His good-nature was often taken advantage of. He has been heard to declare, that nearly one-third of the patients who consulted him never paid their fees. He was a man too independent in spirit to demand what he had a right to claim, and consequently he was much imposed upon. That the profession are much exposed to the tricks of dishonest men, the following anecdotes will testify.

Of the noted Cooke, who died some years ago at Pentonville, many anecdotes have been related, of plans which he practised in order to cheat medical men into gratuitous advice. One of his modes was to attire himself in rags, and ape the pauper. Another was to procure a letter from some dispensary, and to attend there, which he did once for several weeks before he was found out to be a man of immense fortune.

On some occasions, however, he found himself obliged to seek advice *in propriâ personâ*, but even then he went upon a saving plan: at one time, having a complaint in his leg, he applied to a surgeon in his neighbourhood, a Mr. Pigeon, asking him how long it would take to make a cure. The surgeon answered, "A month." This alarmed the miser, who anxiously inquired what would be the medical demand; and on being told by the surgeon, who saw the complaint was trifling, that it would be a guinea, Cooke replied "A guinea! very well; but mark this—a guinea is an immense sum of money; and when I agree upon sums of such magnitude, I go upon the system of no cure no pay; so if I am not cured by the expiration of the month, I am to pay nothing!"

Mr. Pigeon accepted the terms; and by his diligence and surgical skill, would have closed the wound completely some days within the limited space; which the miser observing, and trembling for his gold, was determined to prevent, if possible; and actually procured an irritating plaster, which he put on, so as to extend the period of cicatrizing, which was then going on wholesomely; and was thus enabled, on the last day of the specified term, to show to the surgeon that the wound was still unhealed. The unhappy wretch, proud of his own infamy, had the hardihood to boast of it afterwards, under the cant phrase of "plucking a pigeon."

Even on his death-bed the ruling passion was still strong upon him; for having sent for several medical men, one only would attend; and he having in a few days sent in some medicine, the dying miser at length entreated him to say how long he thought he might live. The candid apothecary honestly said, " perhaps five or six days;" when Cooke, collecting all his strength for the moment, and starting up in his bed, exclaimed, " There! are you not a dishonest man, a rogue, and a robber, to serve me so?" The apothecary, in some surprise, naturally inquired how he deserved those epithets. " How, Sir!" faintly uttered the dying miser, " why, you are no better than a pickpocket, to rob me of my gold, by sending in two draughts a day, to a man that all your physic will not keep alive for six days! begone from my house, and never enter it again."

The celebrated Dupuytren was more successful in obtaining his fees than Dr. Gregory. He was often cheated by his patients, until he had recourse to the following ingenious device:—

He had a faithful servant, who was stationed at the door of the hall. Dupuytren had two bells fixed over the porter's head, communicating with his consulting-room. On bowing the patient out, Dupuytren rung one of the two bells. If the fee was paid, one particular bell was rung, and the servant understood that all was right, and the patient was allowed to depart without any interruption. If the patient forgot the baron's fee, the " no pay" bell was tingled, and the servant understanding the signal, addressed the patient very politely in the following manner :—" Mille pardons, Monsieur, I think you have forgotten to give the baron his fee." "*Ciel !*" exclaims the patient, "*quelle negligence ! le voici avec mille apologies au baron.*" Notwithstanding Dupuytren's immense wealth, he lived in quite a different way from what persons of his rank do in this country. He occupied only one suite of apartments—a floor as we call it— and it was owing to this circumstance that he had it not in his power to prevent a ball from taking place in the room immediately over his head a night or two before he died; and which, it is said, greatly disturbed his dying moments.

Dr. Gregory died April 2, 1821.

DR. JOHN COAKLY LETTSOM must be allowed to tell the particulars of his own early career. In a letter to his friend Dr. Cuming, dated January 13, 1785, he says, " I went to Settle, an apprentice, a fatherless lad. I rode from the house of Samuel Fothergill, at Warrington, alone; and my guardian, when he parted with me, impressed upon my mind his last words: ' Please thy master, and, above all, *please thyself*. If thou turnest out well, I will recommend thee to my brother, the doctor; and never forget that to be good is to be happy.'

" Poor Sutcliff ! once, and only once, wast thou angry with me, and I shall never forget thy words: ' Thou mayest make a physician, but I think not a good apothecary.' My master had never fewer than two apprentices. The one prior to me was very facetious. For some weeks before my arrival, he informed the market-people that an apprentice was coming from a country where the feet of the inhabitants were opposite to those of England. The country people imagined from such discourses, that his antipode walked on his head. The morning after I arrived was the market-day. Our house faced the market, and an immense concourse surrounded the win-

dow, through which I was surveying my new neighbourhood, little suspecting that I was the object of investigation.   In their features were depicted surprise, curiosity;
disappointment, and other passions.   At length I heard a
wise old *codger*, who seemed to have more discernment
than his neighbours, exclaim amongst the crowd, 'Marry!
I think he looks like other folk!' and away he went to
the market, and the company followed, as soon as they
had made the same discovery, by finding that my heels
were under my head!'"

It appears that Abraham Sutcliff was a surgeon
apothecary, established in practice at Settle, in York-
shire.   He was distantly related to S. Fothergill, at that
time Lettsom's guardian.   Sutcliff was an excellent
classical scholar, although self-taught.   Mr. Pettigrew
thus describes his origin :—"About Halifax weaving was
extensively encouraged.   Sutcliff having no patrimony,
received only twelve months' instruction to spell and read
a little English, when he was appointed to the loom; but
the exertion of throwing the shuttle was too hard for his
constitution to bear.   He was asthmatic early in life; and
he suffered so much in the chest from the mechanical
exertion of weaving, as to be obliged to relinquish the
employment.   He had a distant relation at Kendal, of the
name of Ecroyd, an eminent surgeon, to whom he applied
for any species of servitude.   This journey, a distance of
sixty miles, he performed on foot.   At first he was engaged in carrying out medicines and cleaning the shop.
In this town a considerable school was conducted by
Thomas Rebanks.   Young Sutcliff became acquainted
with some of the schoolboys, from whom he borrowed
books, and occasionally procured instruction.   He left
the loom when he was about sixteen years of age, and at
eighteen he had acquired a knowledge of so much Latin
as to enable him to read a prescription, which he also
learned to compound, and at length was permitted to visit
patients for his master.   Having by strict economy saved

a little money, he was allowed by him to visit Edinburgh to attend some of the classes. Here he regularly studied under Professors Monro, Sinclair, Rutherford, &c. In summer he walked back again to his own station, and resumed his services to his indulgent master. For two or three subsequent winters he repeated his perambulations, and became not only a scholar, but a proficient in medical science; and with a view of exercising his abilities independently, he visited the town of Settle, and commenced his professional duties, in a single chamber, practising surgery, midwifery, and pharmacy. He acquired so much celebrity, as to include in his attendance an extent of at least ten miles on every quarter from his residence, at the period when Dr. Lettsom was apprenticed to him."*

"I was born a Quaker," says Lettsom, "and what is still more strange, I was born so within the tropics. I was brought up in notions which encouraged ideas of a favourite people, of a little remnant, of a chosen few, and such like narrow principles. As I loved reading, I acquired the power of thinking; and, considering that all our society together, compared to the universal creation, was in less proportion than a grain of sand to the great globe, I entertained more ample notions of the universal Parent.

"When I came to London (after the termination of five years apprenticeship to Sutcliff) clothed in a long-flapped

---

* After Lettsom had established himself in town, Sutcliff retired from practice in favour of his son; and, on visiting London, he called on his former apprentice, Dr. Lettsom, who advised him to commence practice as a physician. He replied that it was his intention to do so, but he feared it would be difficult to procure a diploma. Upon this Dr. Lettsom presented him with one. "My lad," said Sutcliff, with his eyes suffused with tears of joy, "this is more than I know how to acknowledge."

coat, and carrying on my head a little bob-wig, unknown, and knowing no one, I was revolving, as I walked slowly along Lombard Street, 'what an atom of insignificance am I in this new world!' At this moment a person abruptly interrupted my reveries, by asking, 'Art thou not from Tortola?' 'Yes.' 'I am glad to see thee: wilt thou dine with me?' 'With all my heart, for I am here like Adam, without one associate.' I do not know by what fatality Lord Beezley thus accosted me and took me to his lodging, for we were total strangers. He was some inches taller than me; his coat had large flaps, which added to his height; his arms and legs made up in length what they lacked in circumference.

"I remember once, as he walked up Cheapside, a little impudent boy kept strutting before him, crying out, '*Ladies and gentlemen, make way, make may, make way, the monument is coming.*'

"Beezley never minded this, but kept his pace, throwing his arms about him, and forming a periphery of three yards equilaterally from the centre of motion."

James Beezley, who thus kindly took Dr. Lettsom under his care, was the author of the Defence of the Character of George Fox against Formey.

Lettsom commenced his medical studies in London at St. Thomas's Hospital, under surgeons Cowell, Baker, and Smith, and physicians Akenside, Russell, and Grieve.

It is not our intention to give the minute details of Dr. Lettsom's life. The reader must be satisfied with an outline, containing such anecdotes as we consider illustrative of his character and that of his contemporaries.

It appears that, after spending twelve months in London, Dr. Lettsom returned to the West Indies, to take possession of some little property which had been left him by his father. It consisted of a small portion of land, and fifty slaves: and although, at this period, Lettsom was only possessed of fifty pounds in the world, he, with a feeling of humanity which does him immortal honour, soon after his arrival at Tortola, emancipated the whole of the slaves; thus reducing himself, by an act of justice, to great poverty at the age of twenty-three.

At Tortola, his native place, Lettsom commenced practice; and, in five months, he succeeded in amassing nearly £2,000; half of which he gave to his mother, and with the other half he returned to England, with the view of following in the footsteps of the celebrated Dr. Fothergill. After attending the Edinburgh school for some time, he, at last, graduated as an M. D. at Leyden, on the 20th of June, 1769; and, after marrying a lady of considerable wealth, he commenced practice in London, where he rose to great eminence as a physician and an author. Dr. Lettsom introduced into this country the *Mangel Wurzel*, or *Beta Hybrida*, as he termed it: he also suggested the establishment of the Infirmary at Margate; and many other institutions of a similar character. After the discovery of vaccination by Jenner, Dr. Lettsom was the first person who sent the vaccine lymph across the Atlantic, and consigned it to the fostering care of his friend Dr. Waterhouse, professor of medicine in the University of Cambridge, Massachusetts; from which it spread through the United States. He founded the London Medical Society; assisted in establishing the Royal Jennerian Society; and in promoting the interest and welfare of every charitable institution in the country. He wrote a large number of works and pamphlets, on a variety of subjects, and entered into correspondence with most of the distinguished literary men of the day.

He died, after a short illness, on the 1st of November, 1815.

For a considerable time he maintained the first practice as a physician in the city of London. His professional emoluments were great. In 1783, he received £3,600; in 1784, £3,900; in 1785, £4,015; and in 1786, £4,500.

Mr. Pettigrew observes, had he at this time taken all

the fees that were presented to him, his receipts would have been doubled. In 1800 he received, in fees, £12,000. This was considerably more than Dr. J. Fothergill ever derived from his practice; his highest sum was £5,000 in one year.

The following anecdotes have been related, as illustrative of Lettsom's generosity :—

In 1782, he was sent for to visit an old gentleman, 74 years of age, who resided in the county of Essex. This gentleman had been a great American merchant; he had kept a princely house, and his heart was literally made up of generosity. The American war ruined him; but his creditors, valuing his upright character, permitted him to reside at his house in the country, with a genteel allowance, until his affairs could be settled. The protracted American war destroyed the prospect of retrieving his affairs; his allowance was, therefore, taken away. He fell sick, and consulted Dr. Lettsom. When the Doctor visited him, the gentleman said to him, pointing to his garden, "Those trees I planted, and have lived to see some of them too old to bear fruit. They are part of my family; and my children, still dearer to me must quit this residence, which was the delight of my youth, and the hope of my old age."

The benevolent Doctor, upon quitting the apartment, left, enclosed in a letter, a check to relieve his immediate necessities. He also purchased the house, which was freehold, for £500, and gave it him for life. The poor merchant's health was restored, his garden continued to be the object of his attention, and he daily blessed his worthy benefactor.

Lettsom was by birth and education a Quaker; but by no means a bigot to the peculiar notions entertained by the Society of Friends. He was ready to join with all, without any distinction of sect, in worshipping the great God, feeling the truth of the following sentiment :—

————"True Religion
Is always mild, propitious, and humble;
Plays not the tyrant, plants no faith in blood,
Nor bears destruction on her chariot wheels;
But stoops to polish, succour, and redress,
And builds her grandeur on the public good."

MILLER.

In 1806, Dr. Lettsom determined to enter into serious combat with the quacks, who were then infesting the metropolis; and he prevailed on Phillips, the proprietor of the "Medical Journal," to allow him to insert, in every number of that work, an anonymous article on each of the advertising quacks of the country. Lettsom began with Brodum, the proprietor of the Nervous Cordial, and other furiously advertized preparations; and, without ceremony, charged him with killing thousands by their indiscriminate use: and, to undermine Brodum, stated that he had been a shoe-black at Copenhagen, a Jew vender of oranges, and, finally, a footman to a mountebank. All this might be partly true, but it could not be legally proved in a court of law. Brodum, to whom the costs of a suit were of no importance, set his attorney to work, and Phillips, the printer, and three or four venders, were served with actions for £5,000 damages.

Phillips called on Lettsom, and the whole college, one by one, to enable him to justify, but in vain; for not one could prove that Brodum had even a single swallower of his nostrums. The lawyers held consultations, and the ingenious Garrow was anxious to get his brother-in-law, Lettsom, out of the scrape. In the mean time, Brodum's attorney pressed for proceedings. At length, the editor of a newspaper stept between Phillips and Brodum; the latter agreed to withdraw his actions, and submit to the costs, provided the author was given up; but, if not, then he expected all expenses to be paid without demur; that the author should whitewash him in the next Journal,

under the same signature; and, further, that Phillips and
the newspaper editor should dine with him. Lettsom
gladly paid the two attorney's bills, amounting to 390*l.*
Phillips had a splendid dinner, and the next Medical
Journal contained a high eulogium on the talents and
virtues of Dr. Brodum.

Thus ended Lettsom's campaign against the London
quacks!

An adventure which this celebrated physician once
met with, we find recorded in his own words:—" It was
my lot, a few years ago, to be attacked on the highway
by a genteel-looking person, well mounted, who demanded
my money, at the same time placing a pistol to my
breast. I requested him to remove the pistol, which he
immediately did. I saw his agitation, from whence I
could perceive he had not been habituated to this hazardous practice; and I added that I had both gold and
silver about me, which I freely gave him, but that I was
very sorry to see a young gentleman risk his life in so
unbecoming a manner, which would probably soon termi-
nate at the gallows: that at the best, the casual pittance
gained on the highway would afford but a precarious sub-
sistence; but that if I could serve him by a private assistance, more becoming his appearance, he might farther
command my purse; and, at the same time, I desired him
to accept a card containing my address, and to call upon
me, as he might trust to my word for his liberty and life.
He accepted my address, but I observed his voice faltered;
it was late at night; there was, however, sufficient star-
light to enable me to perceive, as I leaned towards him on
the window of the carriage, that his bosom was overwhelmed with conflicting passions: at length, bending
forward on his horse, and recovering the power of speech,
he affectingly said, 'I thank you for your offer; American
affairs have ruined me;—I will, dear sir, wait upon you.'"

The man kept his word, and Lettsom finding, on inquiry, the account he gave of himself to be correct, after

making an unsuccessful application, in his behalf, to the Commissioners for relieving the American sufferers, presented a memorial on the subject to the Queen, who it is said, procured the man a commission in the army; and his name subsequently appeared on two occasions, in the Gazette, for promotion, on account of good conduct.

The following well-known squib on the doctor was written by some wag :—

> " When any sick to me apply,
>   I physics, bleeds, and sweats' em :
> If after that they choose to die,
>   What's that to me ?
>
> I. LETTSOM."

The following answer to this ridiculous *jeu d'esprit*, was written by his friend Sir M. Martin :—

> " Such swarms of patients do to me apply,
>   Did I not practice, some would surely die;
> 'Tis true, I purge some, bleed some, sweat some,
>   Admit I expedite a few, still many call
>
> I. LETTSOM."

Dr. Lettsom was remarkable for his punctilious attention to cleanliness. He has often been heard to declare that he would sooner relinquish his fee altogether, than have any thing to do with a person who neglected this duty, as he called it. He once offended one of his best patients, who brought her child for him to see, by telling her that the little patient's disease was brought on by allowing particles of dirt to prevent the cutaneous secretion from going on. The lady felt very indignant, and left the doctor's house in a great rage.*

---

* This reminds us of an anecdote of an American physician whom a lady consulted about her child's precious health. Among other things, she inquired if he did not

Though medical knowledge is undoubtedly increased by experience, for, as Shandy says, "an ounce of a man's own knowledge, is worth a ton of other people's," yet that physician is not always the most experienced, who *sees the greatest number of patients.* The understanding does not gallop as fast as the feet do. A physician who is constantly on the trot may see too much, and think too little. Hugh Smith, who was a very popular man in his day, used to arrange his patients very much after the manner of Dr. Last; when he meant to have a holiday, he would say, "I physic all my patients to-day, because I am going into the country to-morrow."* Lettsom, at one period of his practice, was in the habit of seeing more patients than any one physician practising in London; and on showing Dr. William Saunders his long list, one day at a consultation, the latter facetiously said, "My

---

think the *springs* would be useful. "Certainly, Madam," replied the doctor, as he looked at the child, "I have not the least hesitation in recommending the springs—and the sooner you apply the remedy the better." "You really think it would be good for the dear little thing, don't you?" "Upon my word it is the best remedy I know of." "What springs would you recommend, doctor?" "Any will do, Madam, where you can get plenty of soap and water."

* The late Dr. Sutherland, of Bath, when at Paris, attended *L'Hospital de la Charité.* One day he accompanied the physician running through one of the wards to visit the patients, a friar trotting after him with his book in hand, to minute down the prescriptions: the French doctor stops at a bed, and calls out to the patient in it, with the utmost precipitation, *Toussez vous?* then *suez vous? allez vous a la Selle?* then turning round instantly to the friar, "*Purgezle.*" "*Monsieur, il est mort!*" replied the friar. "*Diable! allons!*" said the doctor, and galloped on to the next patient with rapidity.

dear doctor, how do you manage? do you write for them by the dozen? or have you some patent plan for practising by *steam*, my much-esteemed friend?"

In the cold weather, when the poor were out of work, Dr. Lettsom constantly employed them about his grounds. It happened that a gentleman, whose premises adjoined, met the doctor one winter's morning, and upbraided him for keeping so many men in a state of apparent idleness. "True, neighbour," said the doctor, with a smile of complacency, "but who pays them; thou, or I?" The gentleman felt the reproof; and turning on his heel, bade the doctor good morning.

The doctor was in the practice of carrying the produce of his fees carelessly in his coat pocket. His footman, being aware of this, used to make free with a guinea occasionally, while the coat hung up in the passage. The doctor having repeatedly missed his gold, was suspicious of his footman, and took an opportunity of watching him. He succeeded in the detection, and, without even noticing it to the other servants, called him to his study, and coolly said to him, " John, art thou in want of money?" "No," replied John. "Oh! then, why didst thou make so free with my pockets? and since thou didst not want money, and hast told me a lie, I must part with thee. Now, say what situation thou wouldst like abroad, and I will obtain it for thee; for I cannot keep thee; I cannot recommend thee; therefore, thou must go." Suffice it to say, the doctor procured John a situation, and he went abroad.

" I remember at Spa," says Lettsom, "to have been accosted by a beggar, in very classical Latin. I had just been under an Albinus, a Gaubius, and a Van Ruyen, when this language was more familiar to me than it is at present; and I confess I seldom met it purer than in the mouth of the beggar."

In a previous chapter we have given a sketch of the celebrated Dr. MESSENGER MOUNSEY, the eccentric physician of Chelsea Hospital. Since the publication of that portion of the work, we have discovered the following anecdotes of him, which are too good to be omitted :—

At one period, when the doctor was coming from his brother's in Norfolk to London, in the Norwich coach, during the Christmas holidays, the inside of the coach was crowded with game, as presents from the country gentlemen to their friends in town. As there was only room for one passenger, the doctor would gladly have deferred his departure, although his business in town was of an urgent nature; but they refused at the coach-office to return him the money he had paid to secure his seat, so he determined to put up with the inconvenience, and seated himself inside the coach. When daylight had dawned, he perceived that the game was directed to different people; and being disposed to have a little fun at the expense of others, he commenced altering the directions. The pheasants, which were directed to a nobleman, were sent to some tradesman, and *vice versa*, so that the greatest confusion was created at the coach-office, much to the delight of the mischievous doctor.

Mounsey was one day riding with his servant, when he stopped at a village. Seeing the innkeeper at the door, who bowed to him very graciously, he said, he wanted some tea, and added, " I suppose, since the commutation act, you can give me plenty of home-made bread, with good Norfolk fresh butter and cream, for sixpence?" " You had better have added half-a-dozen new-laid eggs into the bargain," said the publican: " but alight, sir, and walk in." The doctor did so, and the host led him into a large room, where there were no windows. " Now, Sir, if you are willing to pay for candles, I will agree to supply you for the proposed sum." The doctor enjoyed the reply as well as the joke, and stopped the whole night as well as the next day with him.—A day or two after-wards, riding over some downs, he observed a shepherd tending his flock, with a new coat on. " Harkee, friend," said the doctor, " who gave you that new coat?" The shepherd, thinking he was a parson, replied, " The same that clothed you—the parish!" The doctor, highly pleased with the answer, rode on a little way, and then desired his servant to go back, and ask the shepherd if he wanted a place, as he wanted a fool. The servant delivered the message. " Tell your master," said the shepherd, " that his living will not support three of us."

Mounsey being the intimate friend of Lord Godolphin, he was in the habit of telling many anecdotes as related by that nobleman, and among others the following one, relative to his grandmother, Sarah, Duchess of Marlborough. In a conversation which Lady Sutherland had with her mother the Duchess, the former observed, " In all the torrent of abuse poured out on your grace, your worst enemies have never called you a faithless wife." " It was no great merit," said the Duchess, as she was turning over the papers afterwards sent to Mallet for her husband's history, " it was no great merit, for I had the handsomest, the most accomplished, and bravest man in Europe for my husband!" " Yet, Madam, you don't say he was without faults?" replied Lady Sutherland. " By no means. I knew them better than he did himself, or even than I do my own. He came back one day from my poor misled mistress Queen Anne, (I believe when he resigned his commission,) and said he had told her that he thanked God, with all his faults, neither *avarice* nor *ambition* could be laid to his charge. When he told me this," continued she, though not in a laughing humour, " I bit my tongue almost through to prevent my smiling in his face."

Dining with Garrick, in company with Dr. Warburton and Dr. Browne (author of Barbarossa), Mounsey was rather grave. " Why so much out of spirits, doctor?" said Garrick. " Oh he is afraid of Dr. Warburton," said Browne. " Afraid of him!" said Mounsey, looking indignantly at both, " No, I may be dull to-day, for how

can it be otherwise from the effects of *this conversation?*
but I assure you I am not afraid of Dr. Warburton, nor
of his man *Jack* either."

Though Mounsey lived in intimacy with Garrick at
the theatre, and at a variety of private tables, Garrick
was not very fond of asking him to his house; and the
reason he gave for it was, to use his own words, "that
the doctor was so great a blackguard, he could not be
sure of him for a moment."   On his promising, however,
to behave himself better for the future, Garrick ventured
to ask him to meet a large party of right honourables
and fashionables at his house in Southampton Street,
where Mounsey figured for some time with his usual wit
and pleasantry, very much to the pleasure and entertainment of the company.   At the second course, the doctor
wished for a piece of roasted chicken, which was at the
upper end of the table, and calling for it to no purpose
several times to Mrs. Garrick, who happened to be engaged in talking to some noble lord at her elbow, he at
last, raising his voice, exclaimed aloud, " You little confounded toad, will you, or will you not, send me the
wing, leg, bit of the breast, or merry-thought, of some of
those chickens?"   The company laughed, but Garrick's
pride was hurt to the quick, in feeling himself so cava-
lierly treated before so many noble personages.   Dr.
Thompson was present on this occasion, and Garrick
protested he would transfer his interest and patronage to
this physician, in consequence of Mounsey's insolence.*

---

* Dr. Thompson, who was a celebrated physician in
his day, was remarkable for two things—viz., the *sloven-*
liness of his person, and his dislike to *muffins*, which he
always reprobated as being very unwholesome.   On his
breakfasting one morning at Lord Melcomb's, when Garrick was present, a plate of muffins being introduced, the
doctor grew outrageous, and vehemently exclaimed,
" Take away the muffins!"   " No, no," said Garrick

Mounsey was the intimate friend of the eccentric Dr. Barker, who at that time practised as an apothecary in Cheapside. It is said that during the great plague of London, four thieves, availing themselves of the public calamity, took that opportunity to plunder the houses of the dead and dying, yet, notwithstanding, escaped the infection themselves. On its being inquired how they thus insured their safety, it was found that they constantly carried about with them sponges dipped in prepared vinegar, which circumstance led the public to suppose that this was a preservative from infection, and all apothecaries sold it under the denomination of "*the four thieves' vinegar.*"

During the prevalence of the influenza, Barker exhibited at his shop window, " The Four Thieves' Vinegar sold here." This being observed by a physician of Foote's acquaintance, who was in the habit of frequenting the shop, he asked the apothecary " how long it was since he took in three partners ?" Barker assured him that he stood alone in the firm of the house. The doctor took him to the window, and showing him the card, recommended him " to deceive the public no longer." Mounsey was in the habit of telling this story with considerable glee.

SIR RICHARD CROFT was a distinguished accoucheur. He married a daughter of Dr. Denman. He went to Paris to attend the Duchess of Devonshire in her confinement, which circumstance partly increased his business on his return to the metropolis. He rose to great eminence in the department of practice to which he directed his mind. He was called in to attend the Princess Charlotte ; and after the fatal termination of the Princess's delivery, the obloquy which it gave rise to, and the disappointment it occasioned, preyed upon his mind to such

---

seizing the plate, and looking significantly at the doctor, " take away the *ragamuffins.*"

a degree, that about three months subsequent to her death he, in a fit of temporary insanity, shot himself in his bed-room.

It was proved, at the inquest held on his body, that since the death of the Princess Charlotte, he had never been free from melancholy and abstraction; and on Dr. Thackeray's asking after one of his patients, he replied, "That he would give five hundred guineas if it were over, rather than have to attend her." On the night of the suicide, he exclaimed to his servant, who complained of being unwell, "What is your agitation compared to mine?" And a few days before, he struck his forehead with much violence, in the presence of Mr. Hollings, and abruptly said to him, "Good God! what will become of me?" His conduct, with reference to the Princess, was much censured at the time; but Dr. Baillie stated that every thing was done by Sir Richard Croft that skill and humanity could suggest. The fatal issue of the case filled his mind with despair, and alarmed his friends for the safety of his intellect. He was heard frequently to ejaculate to himself, "I shall go mad—I shall end my life in a mad-house—I am ruined—Who will place any confidence in me?" As he was driving in his carriage to the Princess when she was taken ill, he observed to a member of his family, "This case will either make me, or ruin me." Poor Sir Richard! he appears to have had a presentiment that *something* was about to happen which would seriously affect his prospects in life. It is said that a few days before he attended his illustrious patient, he fancied he saw the Princess clad in white, glide through his bed-room. Sir Richard was a man of fine and honourable feelings, and was beloved by all who knew him.

Dr. Thomas Bateman, author of the celebrated work on "Cutaneous Diseases," edited by Drs. Willan and A. T. Thompson, was born in 1778. He attended the lectures of Dr. Baillie, who spoke highly of Bateman's talents and industry. His character, both private and professional, is said to have been marked by strict morality and unimpeachable integrity. He has, however, been charged with dissipation, and a leaning towards the doctrines of materialism. At the commencement of his illness, in 1815, he exclaimed, in a paroxysm of pain, to a friend who attended him, " All these sufferings are a just punishment for my long scepticism and neglect of God and religion !" In this conversation he was absurd enough to attribute his sceptical notions to the natural tendency of some of his professional studies. Some time after he said, in allusion to the first of Scott's Essays on the subject of religion, " This is demonstration! complete demonstration !"

Although endowed with extreme sensibility, and the warmest affections, his deportment to strangers was cold and forbidding. On one occasion, he peremptorily refused to prolong a pleasant visit, because, he said to a companion, he had promised he would be home at twelve o'clock, and could not break his word even to a chambermaid.

Dr. Bateman was a most indefatigable student. He was hardly ever without a pen or book in his hand. His work on the Diseases of the Skin, brought him considerable practice. He has been observed to say, that if a medical man wished soon to establish himself in practice, he ought to write a treatise on a practical point connected with medicine. " I have done so," he would say, " and it has succeeded." But Dr. Bateman was well known as a clever experienced physician, prior to the publication of the work in question. This eminent man died in 1820, much regretted by his contemporaries, relations, and friends.

Of the early life of the late Dr. MACKINTOSH we have some very interesting facts on record. When about ten days old, a curious incident occurred to him. His late Majesty, when Duke of Clarence, happened to dine at the barrack at Halifax, to which the father of the late professor was attached. The child was introduced to him in a very novel way. Being put into a large dish, and concealed by the silver cover, he was placed, during the repast, before the gracious prince, whose astonishment may be better conceived than described, when he discovered the nature of the "dainty dish" that had been served up to him. His Royal Highness enjoyed the joke amazingly, laughed heartily, and took the child in his arms, and, kissing it, desired that it should be called after him. The young doctor had unfortunately, however, been previously christened.

Owing to the military profession of his father, the education of the doctor was a wandering one. In his lectures he has been heard to say that he had been at twenty-five different elementary schools. His education was completed at St. Andrews.

From his earliest years Mackintosh displayed an openness of character, and an originality and independence of mind which have conspicuously marked his subsequent career.

At an early age he was bound an apprentice to one of the first surgeons of Edinburgh. It has been said, with reference to this circumstance, that it was his misfortune to be placed under the guidance of a man of a haughty turn of mind, who, instead of encouraging his pupils, and rendering interesting the abstruse principles of science, treated them with every mark of disrespect and unkindness; thus exhibiting a character of mind which is beneath contempt. He was therefore in his studies left to follow the bent of his own mind. Anatomy and chemistry interested him, and he pursued these sciences with great zeal. The enthusiasm which he displayed, in acquiring a knowledge of anatomy, attracted the notice and admiration of the celebrated Monro (secundus) and of Dr. Barclay, who always took a lively interest in his welfare. He early displayed a turn for original investigation, and, accordingly, almost even before he knew the nature of disease, he took every opportunity to observe its phenomenon at the bedside of the patient. He was, at this period of life, seldom known to read a medical and surgical work, because he candidly confessed he did not understand the author's meaning—for this admission we give him credit. -

The education of the doctor was essentially a practical one, and early accustomed him to observe and judge for himself, and to depend upon his own resources. It thus accorded with the bent of his genius; and although by judicious direction his education might have been improved, still the world has had no cause to lament the practical discipline he then underwent. With such early indications of a talent for original investigation, and a love of truth more than of theory, we are at no loss to understand why he afterwards turned out so eminent a pathologist, and so sound a practitioner.

After finishing his education, Dr. Mackintosh was appointed assistant surgeon of artillery. At the period he entered the army, the Egyptian ophthalmia raged to a great extent. He soon observed that the want of success, in the treatment of this disease, arose from the employment of injudicious means. He then suggested that the disease should be treated on the same plan that is adopted in other cases of inflammation; viz., by copious bleeding to fainting, and by abstaining from the use of stimulants during the acute stage. By following the mode of practice laid down by Dr. M., this formidable disease was much more successfully managed than before; and Dr. Mackintosh was much praised for the improvement introduced into this department of surgery.

Being desirous of investigating the nature of yellow fever, intermittent fever, and other diseases of warm climates, he volunteered his services to accompany an expedition then ready to sail for Barbadoes, where it was to be employed on a very arduous and dangerous enterprise.

Dr. M. was appointed surgeon to a battalion; and the general commanding the expedition expressed his satisfaction at having with them a medical officer of such enterprising talents, and whose gentlemanly manner, and pleasing address, had rendered him so great a favourite in the regiment to which he had previously belonged. In this expedition, which was one of the most hazardous and successful during the late ever-memorable war, Dr. M. partook of all its difficulties and dangers; and on more than one occasion narrowly escaped death from the cannon of the enemy. In endeavouring to reach the island, the boat which contained him upset, and went to the bottom. Not being able to swim, he must have been drowned but for the assistance of a sailor. On another occasion a shell exploded in the tent where he was lying ill of a fever, but he was preserved uninjured.

During this eventful struggle his talents shone conspicuously, and his bold and affable spirit were found to encourage the soldier in the field of battle.

Owing to the great labour, physical and mental, which the doctor underwent, he was attacked with fever, and subsequently he was seized with ague. While labouring under this attack, he had an opportunity of patiently studying the nature of this disease; and on himself he first tried the effect of bleeding in the cold stage, which practice he pursued after he had established himself in Edinburgh, and the adoption of which was strongly recommended in his work on the Practice of Physic.

Subsequently to this period he served in South America, and different parts of the globe, with the same high character which has ever distinguished his career. Dr. M. was obliged to return to Europe in consequence of ill health. After residing at Edinburgh for some time, he was sent to the continent of Europe, and was engaged in all those brilliant struggles which so gloriously terminated in the overthrow of Napoleon Bonaparte. He remained with the army of occupation in France till the year 1818, when the troops returned home, and he was allowed to retire on half-pay. He now settled with his family in Edinburgh; more, however, with the view of educating his children than of getting into practice. It was not long before his eminent professional skill began to be appreciated, and patients flocked to his house to have the advantage of his advice. In the year 1822, an epidemic puerperal fever raged in Edinburgh. Dr. Mackintosh made himself conspicuous on this occasion by his unwearied and unremitting exertions in behalf of the sick, and his fame soon spread from one part of the city to the other. He published the result of his experience and practice in this disease, which is considered to exhibit great knowledge of his profession, united with reasoning power of a high order.

Dr. Hamilton replied to Mackintosh's pamphlet on puerperal fever; and to this he made a rejoinder, which is considered a very masterly production.

In consequence of the death of Dr. James Gregory, Dr. Mackintosh, who had already been lecturing on the principles and practice of physic, was petitioned, by upwards of three hundred students of the Royal Infirmary, to offer himself for the vacant chair in the university. The election took place on Monday, the 4th, when, to the astonishment and disappointment of the students, Dr. Bothwick was elected. In the application which the doctor made to the managers of the Royal Infirmary, Edinburgh, he enters into a brief description of his professional career. In alluding to his works, he says, " The first medical work which I published was on Puerperal Fever, in 1822, which was so well received by the profession that it is now out of print. In 1829, I published a work on the Principles of Pathology and Practice of Physic, in two volumes, which has since gone through two editions; and since the first of November last, five hundred copies of the third edition have been sold."

Again, in alluding to his professional services, he says,

" When this city was threatened with cholera, I reluctantly accepted the situation of physician to the Drummond Street Hospital, which was pressed upon me. Having accepted the office, I endeavoured to perform the duties to the best of my abilities. During the first seven months I passed upwards of thirty entire nights in the hospital; and, in addition to visiting it seven or eight times during the day, I generally made a night visit, between the hours of one and three o'clock, A. M. In thus conscientiously discharging the duties which I had undertaken, I, on two different occasions, ran the risk of my life, and the receipts of my practice were materially diminished from the dread which many had of infection, and from my not being in the way when sent for."

Dr. Mackintosh's death was deeply deplored by a large and respectable circle of friends, to whom he was much endeared.

CHESELDEN, the eminent surgeon and anatomist, came before the public at an earlier period of life than almost any other in the long list of professional excellence. He was a fellow of the Royal Society at twenty-one years of age, and at twenty-two gave lectures on surgery! He was truly master of his art, which he simplified, improved, and ornamented. Living at a period, considered as an intellectual era in this country, he was the companion and friend of the "great master-spirits of the age," the men of genius and taste.

He acquired great fame by giving sight to a boy who was born blind; but what distinguished him most, was his skill in performing the operation of lithotomy. Persons came from all parts of the world for his professional assistance; and the arrival of a distinguished foreigner is thus announced, in May, 1734:—" Baron Carlson, Secretary of State to the King of Sweden, lately arrived here for that purpose, was cut for the stone, at the house of Baron Sparr, by W. Cheselden, who took from him, in *two minutes and four seconds*, two stones, each as big as a large walnut, and three of a smaller size."

Cheselden has been said to have been vain of his acquirements. Be that as it may, he was a charitable and a good man; he belonged to many public charities; and when the Foundling Hospital was first proposed, he sent a benefaction with two lines from Pope:

" 'Tis what the happy to the unhappy owe;
  For what man gives, the gods by him bestow."

In the beginning of 1736, Cheselden was thus honourably mentioned by Pope, " As soon as I had sent my last letter, I received a most kind one from you, expressing great pain for my late illness at Mr. Cheselden's. I conclude you were eased of that friendly apprehension in a few days after you had despatched yours, for mine must have reached you then. I wondered a little at your question, who Cheselden was. It shows that the truest merit does not travel so far any way as on the wings of poetry: he is the most noted, and most deserving man in the whole profession of chirurgery; and has saved the lives of thousands by his manner of cutting for the stone."

He appears to have been on terms of intimate friendship with Pope, who frequently, in his letters to Mr. Richardson, talks of dining with Cheselden, who then lived in or near Queen Square.*

Another proof of his intimacy arises from a poem of the younger Richardson, sent to Pope at Twickenham, after being declared out of danger by his physicians, in which we are told that,

" Cheselden, with candid wile,
Detains his guest; the ready Lares smile.

---

* " I'll do what Mead or Cheselden advise."
Pope—Imitation of Horace, p. 39.

Good Chiron too, within his welcome bower,
Received of verse the mild and sacred power;
With anxious skill supplied the blest relief,
And healed, with balms, and sweet discourse, his grief."

Cheselden's manners were extremely kind and gentle;
and notwithstanding the extensive practice he had been
engaged in, he always, before an operation, felt sick
at the thoughts of the pain he was about to inflict; though
during its performance, his coolness and presence of mind
never forsook him. In alluding to this feeling, Moraud
relates an anecdote of a French surgeon, who, on visiting
the hospital, expressed great surprise at witnessing such
an evidence of weakness, as he considered it, on the part
of so famous a surgeon. After the operation was over,
the visiter was invited by Cheselden to accompany him
to the fencing-school, whither he was going to see a
sparring-match; but here the tables were completely
turned, for no sooner did the contest begin, than the
stranger turned pale at the sight, and was obliged speedily
to betake himself to the open air.

A relation of this eminent physician was condemned
to be hanged. Cheselden proposed, if the king would
pardon him, to take out the drum of the prisoner's ear, in
order to try what effect it would have; and if it succeeded, the experiment was to be repeated on Lady Suf-
folk. The man was pardoned, but the operation was never
performed!

Cheselden had considerable taste in matters of art:
the plan of Fulham Bridge was drawn by him. In the
frontispiece to Cheselden's great work on the Bones, is
the figure of Belchier in his morning-gown, and Sharp,
is the young man behind him. Cheselden is not represented himself. It is stated that this distinguished surgeon lost 1700l. by this work, as so many of the expensive
plates were cancelled, and alterations made while he was
about it. Douglass, who wrote a peevish intrigue upon

it, called Belchier up one morning at six o'clock, when the work was published, and asked him if Cheselden was mad, by saying that he had not room enough to write more on the bones. "What!" said he, "could he not get more paper."

Of the illustrious surgeon, Pott, a short notice must be given. MR. PERCIVAL POTT was originally intended for the church, in which he had considerable prospect of preferment; but he resisted the importunities of his friends, having manifested, in early life, a strong propensity for the profession to which he was destined in after-life to become so bright an ornament. In 1736, Pott commenced practice in Fenchurch Street. In 1749, he was appointed one of the principal surgeons of St. Bartholomew's Hospital. At this period the state of the science of surgery was still very imperfect, notwithstanding some sensible and ingenious men had published observations which had enlightened and improved it. Still the maxim, " *Dolor medecina doloris,*" remained unrefuted; the severe treatment of the old school, in the operative part of surgery, continued in force; the first principles of the science, the natural process and powers of healing, were either not understood, or not attended to; painful escharotic dressings were continually employed; and the actual cautery was in such frequent use, that, at the times when surgeons visited the hospital, it was regularly heated and prepared in the wards of the hospital and in the presence of the patients, as a part of the necessary apparatus. Mr. Pott lived to see these remains of barbarism set aside, and a more humane and rational plan, of which he was the originator, universally adopted.

An accident which Pott met with made him an author. As he was riding he was thrown from his horse, and suffered a compound fracture of his leg, the bone being forced through the integuments. Conscious of the danger attendant on fractures of this nature, and thoroughly aware how much they may be increased by rough treatment or improper position, he would not suffer himself to be moved until he had made the necessary dispositions. He sent to Westminster for two chair-men to bring their poles; and patiently lay on the cold pavement, it being the middle of January, until they arrived. In this situation he purchased a door, to which he made them nail their poles. When all was ready, he caused himself to be laid on it, and was carried through Southwark, over London Bridge, to Watling Street, where he was then living—a tremendous distance in such a state! It was during his confinement in consequence of this accident, that he planned and partly executed his celebrated treatise on Ruptures.

In 1760, he published his work on the Injuries to which the Head is liable from external violence; a publication which placed his name in the highest rank as a writer, and as an able surgeon. He was much engaged in practice at this time; and in order to collect many facts bearing upon the subject of his treatise, he was in the practice of visiting, almost daily, every hospital in London; and entered into a correspondence with the most eminent continental surgeons. "I must have facts," he would say: "what are mere opinions worth; any man may give an opinion, but it is not every mind that is qualified to collect and arrange important facts?"

Pott possessed a kind and humane disposition. He was ever ready to lend a helping-hand to medical men in distress. At one period he had three surgeons, who had been reduced in circumstances, living in his own house, until he could find means by which they could earn an independent livelihood. He was most kind and attentive to the patients in the hospital: in particular cases, he was not satisfied with seeing them at the ordinary periods, but he visited the hospital several times during the day. On one occasion, he had performed a complicated and dangerous operation. He had seen the patient three times during the day; and during the following night he dreamed that the assistant at the hospital had forgotten to administer a particular medicine that he had ordered, and from which he had anticipated much good effect. He could not remain easy whilst this impression was on his mind. He rose from his bed, dressed himself, and in the middle of the night, without disturbing any of the family, went to the hospital, gained admission, had the house-surgeon summoned to his side, in order to satisfy himself that his instructions had been punctually obeyed. To his great astonishment, he found that the medicine had not been exhibited! Pott always declared that his dream had saved his patient's life.—Although a great surgeon and skilful operator, Pott was nervous prior to performing any difficult operation. He never allowed a day to pass without dissecting some portion of the human body. He considered it the sacred duty of every surgeon who might be called upon to operate upon the living, to be always operating upon the dead. This was his practice, and he strongly recommended it to others.

The retirement of Sir Cæsar Hawkins from London practice, was the means of considerably enlarging Pott's connexions. He then lived in Hanover Square.

Pott died on the 23d of December, 1788. On the last day of his illness he observed, " My lamp is almost extinguished; I hope it has burned for the benefit of others."

The person of Mr. Pott was elegant, though less than the middle size; his countenance animated and expressive; his manners and deportment were graceful; and his remarkable vigour and activity seemed unabated by age. He was distinguished as a surgeon for his sound judgment, cool determination, and great manual dexterity.

MR. WILLIAM HEY was a most distinguished surgeon. He commenced his studies at the place of his birth, Leeds, and came to London in 1757, and placed himself under the tuition of the most able masters of his day. He studied under Broomfield, and Dr. Donald Monro of St.

George's Hospital. During the period which Mr. Hey devoted to the study of his profession in London, he undertook, says Mr. Pearson, the very difficult task of governing his thoughts; and perhaps very few persons ever exercised such a perfect control over them as he was enabled to do, from those early days of his youth to the end of his life. He determined that he would meditate upon a given subject, while he was walking a certain distance, and that then he would turn his attention to some other topic; and he was thus accustomed to pass through the streets of London investigating the various subjects to which his thoughts had been directed by the lectures, or other professional occupations. The effect of this habit remained with him through life; and he found it of admirable use, not only in preserving him from the intrusion of a swarm of impertinent ideas, but in enabling him to form a correct judgment on many points pertaining to divine and human knowledge.

After finishing his education in London he returned to Leeds, where he immediately established himself in practice. He soon rose to great eminence in his profession. At the establishment of the Leeds Infirmary, he was unanimously elected the principal surgeon of the institution, which office he filled for many years, with great credit and honour to himself, and advantage to the patients admitted under his care. He was also appointed Mayor of Leeds, in consequence of the celebrity which his talents had enabled him to acquire. Mr. Hey was as distinguished for his piety as for his professional skill. He was beloved and respected by all who had the high privilege of being acquainted with him. At the age of eighteen, he joined the Methodists, who were under the direction and superintendence of the Rev. J. Wesley, and he continued in connexion with them for twenty or thirty years. Mr. Hey left behind many records of his professional exertions. His "Surgical Observations," is still a standard medical work. He was a skilful operator—in fact, he possessed all the qualifications necessary to constitute a good surgeon. He invariably retired to a room to offer up a prayer to the Divine Being, previous to his performing any operation, and he attributed his success in the use of the knife to this circumstance.

In domestic life he was kind, tender, and affectionate—as a magistrate, just, legal, and conscientious. In him virtue and religion found a father and a protector—vice, a stern but merciful judge and monitor. His surgical writings, which will be studied by the faculty as long as true knowledge of their profession is an object, evince a strong, comprehensive, and enlightened view of those subjects which he undertook to illustrate.

Mr. Hey died in March, 1819.

JAMES HEAVISIDE was born at Hatfield, where his father was a general practitioner, much esteemed by the neighbouring gentry, and particularly patronised by the Duke of Leeds and Lord Salisbury. "I had the pleasure," says the writer from whom we have borrowed the particulars of our sketch of this eminent surgeon, "of making Heaviside's acquaintance very early in life, and received many civilities from him, partly from that urbanity which was natural to him, and partly from some friendly recollections of a very near and dear relation, with whom he was fellow-pupil under Mr. Pott." Heaviside commenced his professional career in Mortimer Street, Cavendish Square; where having more leisure time than was good for his health, his father thinking that horse-exercise would benefit it, purchased for him a surgeoncy in the Life-Guards. Shortly after, he became a candidate for the office of assistant-surgeon to St. Bartholomew's Hospital; and though he did not succeed, it must be remembered, to his credit, that he did not canvass for it—a point of honour not so scrupulously attended to by his opponents. When his father died, he came into a fortune, on which he might have retired; but his character displayed itself, and he evinced his love for the profession by forming his museum, which for many years attracted public curiosity, and at last excited professional attention and jealousy; as some were pleased to think, that

> "With coffee, tea, and butter'd rolls,
>   He found an easy way to people's souls;"

and which the envious insisted, pertained more to the nature of a discovery in philosophy than physiology. Amongst the qualifications that fit a man for the important duties of a professional life, may be ranked punctuality, attention, assiduity, and gentleness; all of which Mr. Heaviside possessed in an eminent degree, and they doubtlessly contributed largely to his success. He may be said to have lived in surgery for half a century. He never left London for recreation; and was always forthcoming, whenever an emergency required his presence. His domestic staff was well appointed, and his zealous aide-de-camp, who was his valet for thirty years, never failed to produce his master at any hour of the day and night; which, perhaps, may furnish us with a reason why he was so frequently called in to cases of accidents, and consequently so often figured as a witness in the courts of justice. "Egad," said Jekyl one day, "we never have a *homicide*, or a *suicide*, or any other *cide*, without a *Heaviside!*"

The principal event in his life arose out of his professional attendance at the fatal duel between Colonel Montgomery and Captain Macnamara, in 1802. For this he was committed to Newgate, and during a whole fortnight subjected to much pain and anxiety. His friends, Messrs. Erskine and Garrow, Mr., afterwards Baron Wood, and others, volunteered their aid; but still, the dread of the capital punishment, and with it the forfeiture of his property, made his situation seriously uncomfortable. In this dilemma, his brokers, Messrs. Johnson and Langden, sold out his stock, which, together with the rest of his possessions, was conveyed to a third party in safety; and to the credit of these gentlemen it should be told, that, though the amount must have been an object to be desired, yet, under the circumstances of the case, they transacted the business without the charge of a single farthing. In the end, the grand jury ignored the bill against Mr. Heaviside.

This surgeon died on the 19th of September, 1828, much regretted by a large circle of admiring friends.

CHAPTER VIII.

MAD DOCTORS, AND MAD-HOUSES.

Importance of the subject—Instruction to Medical Witnesses—
Curious cases of insanity showing the cunning of lunatics—
Remarkable mental delusions—A visit to a mad-house.

THE subject upon which we are now entering is one of
the highest interest—both to the medical world, and to the
whole community; inasmuch as are included within it,
not only questions of physiology, pathology, and medical
jurisprudence, but likewise those which involve the liberty
and happiness of every member of society. When called
upon to decide in a case of ordinary disease, the physician
may err in judgment, and his error may be productive of
great evil to the patient: his life may be jeopardized, or
at least his health may be irrecoverably damaged; but if
he errs in judging a case of suspected insanity, he not
only perils the life and health of his patient, but his very
liberty. Upon his decision, the man is to be either restored to the rank and privilege of a rational and responsible being, or to be subjected to those moral and physical
restraints, which the law has deemed necessary to throw
around the lunatic, for the protection of himself, his property, and the society in which he moves. It may be
urged that whatever is the primary effect of a physician's
opinion, in a case of suspected insanity—the ulterior proceedings and their results are not consequent upon his
decision, but upon the verdict of a jury. But let it be
remembered that the first step in the inquisition must be

taken by the physician ; he is called to examine the case, and without his certificate, the patient cannot be consigned to a mad house ;—by his report to the Lord Chancellor, when required to send him an opinion of the case, his lordship is guided in his decision, whether to dismiss the petition or to send the case to a jury ;—and, lastly, when the writ *De Lunatico Inquirendo* is issued, the judgments of the commissioners and jury must be almost entirely governed by the evidence of the medical witnesses. How important then is the investigation of mental disease ; and yet it is a melancholy fact, that there are no affections so little understood, or that have received so little attention, as diseases of the intellectual powers. It is astonishing how various have been the theories of insanity, and how much ignorance and quackery have been, until a very recent period, exhibited in the treatment of the insane. At one period they were considered under satanic influence, and driven away from the abodes of men. Afterwards they were supposed to be affected by lunar changes, which opinion gave origin to the term lunatic, and prevails to this day to a great extent among the ignorant. Then it was supposed that the malady was not a bodily affection, but one which had seized upon the spiritual part, and therefore placed beyond the reach of physical remedies, so that medical treatment was regarded as altogether useless ;—to this opinion is owing the neglect into which these investigations had fallen, and the discreditable ignorance of the great body of practitioners upon the subject of insanity. Of late years, however, great advances have been made, by improved theories and practice, towards both the comfort and restoration of the insane ; and physicians are becoming more and more convinced of the value of medicine as a remedial agent in the cure of insanity. Still, however, it cannot be denied that this disease, in common with most of the class of nervous affections, is involved in great obscurity, of which we have a melancholy proof in almost every case where a judicial investigation is necessary. Lawyers are too apt to regard an inquiry into the state of a lunatic's mind as they would a case at *nisi prius;* and because of their fee, they deem it necessary to bring all the pettifogging trickery of their profession, to bear down if possible the opposing testimony; and knowing the obscurity of the subject, and the difficulties which medical men have to contend with, in arriving at a correct opinion, they most unfairly in their examination, endeavour to tie them down to definitions, and then, by showing their fallacy, weaken the whole effect of their testimony. An honest lawyer should remember, that he, with the commissioners, jury, and witnesses, have only one object, viz., the interest of the unfortunate lunatic : if he be of unsound mind, and incapable of managing himself and his affairs—doubtless humanity urges the necessity of all legal protection and restraint; but, if he be still, notwithstanding some eccen-tricity of conduct, a rational and responsible being, no fee, or reward, or party, should induce a man to mystify the subject, or obstruct, by skilful pleading or ingenious quibbling, the progress of truth. As however all lawyers will not be guided by such pure feelings toward the sub-ject of their investigation, it is necessary for medical men to guard themselves well against any admissions which may, by a skilful advocate, be turned against them. As was before remarked, there is nothing so eagerly seized upon, as a definition—therefore the witness should be very cautious in committing himself by attempting to define insanity; and it will be wiser and better at once to ac-knowledge his incapacity to do so—than by a vain and ostentatious display of metaphysical lore, to peril the interest of a fellow-creature.

The medical witness is called upon to say, from his previous examination of the case, and from the facts which have been brought before him, during the investigation in court, whether the supposed lunatic be of unsound mind, and incapable of managing himself and his affairs, with or without lucid intervals; and, lastly, if unsound, when that unsoundness commenced. The term unsound mind, it must be confessed is one of the worst that could have been devised to denote that condition of mind which requires legal restraint, as it may include almost every variety and degree of mental disorder—from imbecile judgment to confirmed insanity. But the medical witness has nothing to do with the legal definition of the term. All that is required of him is to determine whether there exists, or has existed, such a morbid condition of the intellectual powers, as unfits a man for the management of himself or his affairs; and it is not necessary that he should have proof of want of judgment and discretion in the control of his affairs, in order to judge him unfit for such control; but he may infer such unfitness from the existence of depraved intellect. The great question for the physician's examination therefore is—does a morbid condition of the intellect exist; and when did it commence; and have there been, during its existence, any lucid intervals? In conducting his examination, the physician must never forget the exceeding cunning and subtlety often displayed by lunatics, in evading the evidence, and artfully concealing his real opinions and feelings. A curious case, tried before Lord Mansfield, may be adduced in illustration of this fact. A man named Wood, had indicted Dr. Monro for false imprisonment in a mad-house—he being sane. The plaintiff underwent a most severe examination by the defendant's counsel, without exposing his complaint; but Dr. Battie having come upon the bench, and having desired the judge to ask him what was become of the Princess whom he had corresponded with in cherry-juice, he showed in a moment his delusion, by answering that there was nothing at all in that, because having been (as every body knew) imprisoned in a high tower, and being debarred the use of ink, he had no other means of correspondence but by writing his letters in cherry-juice, and throwing them into the river which surrounded the tower, where the Princess received them in a boat. There existed of course, no tower, no imprisonment, no writing in cherry-juice, no river, no boat: but the whole the inveterate phantom of a morbid imagination. I immediately (continued Lord Mansfield) directed Dr. Monro to be acquitted; but this man Wood, being a merchant in Philpot Lane, and having been carried through the city in his way to the mad-house, indicted Dr. Monro over again, for the trespass and imprisonment in London, knowing that he had lost his cause by speaking of the Princess at Westminster : and such (said Lord Mansfield) is the extraordinary subtlety and cunning of madmen, that when he was cross-examined on the trial in London, in order to expose his madness, all the ingenuity of the bar, and all the authority of the court, could not make him say a single syllable upon that topic, which had put an end to the indictment before, although he still had the same indelible impression on his mind, as he signified to those who were near him; but conscious that the delusion had occasioned his defeat at Westminster, he obstinately persisted in concealing it.

Lord Erskine, in defending Hatfield, who was tried for shooting at George the III. in Drury Lane Theatre, in 1800,* mentioned a very striking instance of the cunning with which madmen sometimes stifle the disorder. Lord

---

* This unfortunate man had a child eight months old, of which he was passionately fond. On the day on which he attempted the life of the King, he went to the bed-side of the mother, who had the infant in her arms; and while the tears of affection for his offspring ran down his face, he seized it, and endeavoured to dash out its brains against the wall. This man was perfectly conscious that he was the husband of the woman, and the father of the child; he knew that it was criminal to perform the act which he contemplated; but he acted " under the overruling dominion of a morbid imagination."

Erskine had wasted a whole day in a vain endeavour to demonstrate to the judge and jury the insanity of an unfortunate gentleman who had brought an action against his brother and the keeper of a mad-house for confining him in a mad-house when he asserted his perfect sanity. He replied so well to Lord Erskine's queries, that the judge, the jury, and the audience believed that he was sane, and the victim of wanton oppression. At last Dr. Sims came into court, and suggested to Lord Erskine to inquire whether he did not believe himself to be *Jesus Christ?* Lord Erskine took the hint, and pretended to lament his ignorance, and the indecency of his examination; the poor gentleman expressed his forgiveness, and with the utmost gravity, in the face of the whole court, emphatically exclaimed, "I am the *Christ?*" and so the cause ended.

There are two modes of establishing this morbid state of the faculties; first, by showing the presence of a specific delusion—and secondly, by proving the existence of a series, of extravagancies in opinion or conduct. The first is the most conclusive evidence which can be adduced; and when proved, carries conviction at once to the mind of the jury.

When the proof depends upon the existence of a series of extravagancies, the physician must guard himself against a trick which lawyers sometimes practice in order to overturn the effect of this species of evidence. The witness has detailed a series of extravagant conduct, and has inferred therefrom the mental unsoundness of the patient; and, taken collectively, it may be as strong and unanswerable as any other description of evidence; but, in the cross-examination of the witness, the counsel by a species of legal analysis, skilfully separates the whole conduct of the patient into detached portions, and putting each extravagance *seriatem* to the witness, inquires whether it is a proof of unsoundness; and thus may he be reduced to the necessity of renouncing his opinion, or of absurdly maintaining it, after all the evidence upon which it was based, has been knocked away. We have known a medical witness brought into this humiliating predicament by the ingenuity of counsel, because he had not nerve enough to explain, that the force of his evidence did not depend upon any single act of extravagance, but upon the whole conduct of the patient taken collectively.

We cannot better illustrate our views than by adding some cases of remarkable delusion, by which it will be shown that the utmost cunning and care are often necessary to enable the practitioner to detect aberration of mind.

A gentleman who was insane, and had long been the inmate of a mad-house, wrote to his friends that he had recovered his senses, and although he was perfectly aware that he had been properly shut up, yet now that he was well, he trusted they would no longer force him to associate with madmen, and suffer all the miseries of the place in which he was confined. A clergyman and physician were sent to examine him, and their report was favourable to his sanity : his friends appointed a day to restore him to liberty and society. They went to the asylum, and were rejoiced to hear him converse so sensibly, that no doubt of his sanity existed in their minds, and they prepared to take him with them. As the party descended the stairs of the mad-house, a half-naked madman, in one of the cells called out, with a loud voice, " where are you taking that madman ? You shall repent of your folly,—for I am Neptune, I shall prevent any rain from falling upon the earth for many weeks, so that your crops will be burnt up and utterly destroyed." The madman whom the party was removing, looked round upon the poor maniac who had uttered this threat, with an expression of extreme contempt. " Do not regard his threat," said he, speaking to his friends, " he says he is

NEPTUNE! well, I am JUPITER, and I can make it rain whenever I please."

A celebrated watch-maker, at Paris, was infatuated with the chimera of perpetual motion; and to effect this discovery, he set to work with indefatigable ardour. From unremitting attention to the object of his enthusiasm, coinciding with the influence of revolutionary disturbances, his imagination was greatly heated, his sleep was interrupted, and, at length, a complete derangement of the understanding took place. His case was marked by a most whimsical illusion of the imagination. He fancied that he had lost his head on the scaffold; that it had been thrown promiscuously among the heads of many other victims; that the judges having repented of their cruel sentence, had ordered those heads to be restored to their respective owners, and placed upon their respective shoulders; but that, in consequence of an unfortunate mistake, the gentleman, who had the management of that business, had placed upon his shoulders the head of one of his unhappy companions. The idea of this whimsical exchange of his head occupied his thoughts night and day, which induced his relatives to send him to the Hôtel Dieu: from thence he was transferred to the Asylum de Bicêtre. Nothing could exceed the extravagance and ridiculousness of the notions which had taken possession of his imagination. He sung, cried, or danced incessantly; and, as there appeared no propensity in him to commit acts of violence or disturbance, he was allowed to wander about the hospital unrestrained, in order to expend, by evaporation, the effervescent excess of his spirits. " Look at these teeth," he constantly cried; " mine were exceedingly handsome—these are rotten and decayed. My mouth was sound and healthy—this is the reverse. This is not my hair; this is not my nose; my cheeks were ruddy—these are pale and ghastly."

It is to this extraordinary case that Moore alluded in his, " Fudge Family in Paris."

" Went to a mad-house,—saw a man
   Who thinks, poor wretch, that, while the Fiend
Of Discord here full riot ran,
   He, like the rest was guillotin'd ;—

But that when, under BONEY's reign,
   (A more discreet, though quite as strong one)
The heads were all restored again,
   He, in the scramble, got a *wrong one.*

Accordingly he still cries out,
   ' This strange head fits me most unpleasantly ;'
And always runs, poor dev'l, about,
   Inquiring for his own incessantly !"

In going round the wards of a large asylum, not far from the city of London, we entered a room where we saw a number of lunatics seated on each side of a long table. We sat down by a young man who had a very intelligent expression of countenance. He looked at us, and after bowing and saying, " How do ye do," he exclaimed, " I am the king !" " Are you ?" we replied, " we had no idea that we had the honour of sitting so near majesty." " Oh, yes, I am the king," he continued, " I have cured three hundred patients since I have been here. We have a grand feast to-night. I shall let them all out of the house. Will you come here this evening ?" We questioned the lunatic as to what he intended to do. He said he was going to build a house up to heaven, and then asked if we thought Christ would be angry. He promised us a seat next to the queen, and he appeared much delighted at our consenting to visit him in the evening.

We had a long conversation with a woman who imagined herself to be the Queen of the Belgians. She thought that Prince Leopold had treated her with great cruelty. She was convinced she was his lawful wife, and wished to know if we would promise to let the king know where she was, and how shamefully she was treated. On our promising to comply with her request she appeared satisfied.—In the same institution we saw an interesting case of mania caused by religious excitement. The poor youth, who was remarkably interesting in appearance, was always engaged in prayer. The first thing he would do in the morning, was to go into one corner of the ward and stand over a sink, where he would remain the greater part of the day engaged in fervent prayer. No entreaties could induce him to abandon this practice.

Esquirol, in his work on the "Illusions of the Insane," relates several interesting cases which have formed the basis of some important observations relating to the treatment of insanity.

The famous Térouane de Méricourt lived ten years at the Salpétrière in a state of madness. She used to throw two pails of water on her bed every morning and evening, and lie down immediately afterwards. "I have seen her," says Esquirol, "break up the ice to procure water from the fountains."

An artillery officer, twenty-seven years of age, of a sanguineous temperament, and of a strong athletic form, was seized with an intermittent fever during the Prussian campaign. They made him swallow a large glass of brandy, into which they had mixed the gunpowder of two cartridges. He became mad immediately, and tore up every thing that fell in his way, linen, wearing apparel, and bed-clothes; they were obliged to let him sleep upon straw. Feeling himself pricked, he placed the straw in a ring, leaving in the centre an empty space, which he occupied; he now moved his head in every direction, blowing incessantly upon the straw, which surrounded him, and screaming from time, as if to drive away menacing objects. This symptom continued night and day for more than three weeks. It was then discovered that he mistook the straws for the beaks of birds of prey that had wounded him. He blew upon the straw, and screamed in order to frighten away these annoying animals. Subsequently the same patient had new illusions of a still more extraordinary character.

A general officer, more than fifty years old, who had suffered from rheumatism during the war, was seized with furious madness after some domestic trials. His teeth were bad, and he suffered much from them. He attributed the pains he felt to the sun, and when they were very acute, he screamed in a most frightful manner, and threatened to exterminate the sun with his brave troops. Sometimes the pains attacked one knee; he would then seize with one hand the afflicted part, and with the other hand closed would strike it violently, calling out, "Wretch! thou shalt not escape." He fancied he had a thief in that knee.

A woman, about fifty-seven years of age, of a strong constitution had been porteress at the nunnery of Notre-Dame, and was very devout. The events of the revolution with other circumstances connected with her bodily health, concurred to deprive her of reason, and she was taken to the Salpétrière, where she lived a great number of years. She was of small size, had a thick and short neck, and large head, and her countenance had something mysterious about it. She was called the "mother of the church," because she spake incessantly on religious subjects. She fancied she had in her inside all the personages of the New Testament, and sometimes those of the Bible. She would frequently exclaim, "I can bear it no longer! when will there be peace in the church?" If her pains became more acute, she would add, with imperturbable coolness, "They are crucifying Jesus Christ to-day; I hear the blows of the hammer as they drive in the nails." She imagined also that the pope held a council in her abdomen, and nothing could dissipate these ludicrous illusions. Upon the death of

this patient, considerable structural disease was discovered in the abdominal cavity.

"We have," says Esquirol, "at Charenton, a monoma-
niac who fancies he is conducted to the cellars of the
opera every night, and that there, and sometimes in his
own room, they stab him with poniards in his back and
chest; then they cut off sometimes one of his arms, at
other times one of his thighs, and sometimes even his
head. When this unfortunate man is reminded that his
head is on his shoulders, that he still possesses his limbs,
and that his body displays no wounds, he answers, " They
are witches, conjurors, and freemasons, who possess the
secret of putting limbs on again, without its being perceived." If they insist upon it, he says, " You side with
these monsters and brigands; kill me! kill me! I cannot bear their cruelty, nor resist the sufferings which
they make me endure."

There is a patient confined in an asylum in the vicinity
of London, whose insanity was caused by the political
excitement which took place after the rejection of the
Reform Bill, by the House of Lords. This man was
actively engaged in promoting the establishment of the
great political union, in London, and it was during this
period that he evinced decided symptoms of mental aberration. His delusion took a singular turn. He fancied,
and still fancies, himself a candidate for a seat in parliament. He occasionally mounts a bench, and harangues
in the most impassioned manner the other lunatics in the
ward. He tells them to send him to the House of Commons, to represent their interests, by their unbought and
unsolicited suffrages. We are told by a medical gentleman who has seen this case, that he affords considerable
amusement to the inmates of the asylum. He is most
violent in his abuse of the House of Lords, for rejecting
the " people's bill," as he terms it. This is his only delusion: when he is not engaged in speaking to the doctors, he is usually employed in writing addresses and

advertisements. The gentleman under whose care he is placed, has frequently endeavoured to persuade him that the Reform Bill was carried, and is now the law of the land. He laughs at the assertion, and says " it is a weak invention of the enemy." A *fracas* took place in the ward one afternoon, in consequence of a lunatic, who had just been admitted, and who of course, was unacquainted with the morbid delusion of this man, refusing to promise to vote for him. The would-be M. P. swore at him, made use of every opprobrious epithet he could think of, and at last commenced pummelling the lunatic. The other patients thought this an unparliamentary course of procedure, and took the poor man's part, and the result was, that the " reformer," was compelled to beat a retreat in order to escape the punishment which his conduct so richly deserved.

The following affecting case is recorded by Mr. Hill. A gentleman, on the point of marriage, left his intended bride for a short time; he usually travelled in the stage-coach to the place of her abode; the last journey he took from her, was the last of his life. Anxiously expecting his return, she went to meet the vehicle. An old friend announced to her the death of her lover. She uttered an involuntary and piteous exclamation, " he is dead !" From that fatal moment, for *fifty years*, has this unfortunate female daily, in all seasons, traversed the distance of a few miles, to the spot where she expected her future husband to alight from his coach, uttering, in a plaintive tone, " He has not come yet—I will return to-morrow."

THE END.

CONTENTS

OF THE

HOME & TRAVELLER'S

LIBRARY.

No. I.—TEXAS AND THE GULF OF MEXICO; OR, YACHTING IN THE NEW WORLD. By Mrs. Houstoun. With Illustrations. Price 25 Cents.

"An excellent and entertaining work."—*U. S. Gazette.*

No. II.—THE ENGLISHWOMAN IN EGYPT. By Mrs. Poole. With an Engraving of the Interior of the Great Pyramid. Price 25 Cents.

"The first English lady who has been admitted as a privileged friend into the hareems of those of the highest rank in the Egyptian Capital."—*Blackwood's Magazine.*

"All feeling of tediousness is lost in the single wish that there was more."—*Smith's Weekly Volume.*

"The excellent little book which results from Mrs. Poole's observations, gives us, in a few pages, more information on the grand mystery of Oriental homes, than we have ever been able to draw from other sources."—*London Quarterly Review.*

"All the men in Europe together could never have gained or imparted the information in this book."—*London Morning Post.*

"Emphatically the book of a *lady*."—*Frazer.*

" Informing, sprightly, and entertaining."—*New Monthly.*

" The first good book on Egypt by a lady."—*Tait.*

" Most agreeable and entertaining."—*Chambers.*

No. III.—NIGHTS OF THE ROUND TABLE. By Mrs. Johnstone, author of " Clan Albyn," " Elizabeth De Bruce," &c. Price 25 Cents.

" This book, the third of the series entitled ' The Home and Traveller's Library,' is a collection of pleasant stories, of a kind calculated to do good, as well as to amuse. This volume strengthens the good opinion already formed of the library. If the publishers proceed as they have commenced, they will give families one of the most valuable cabinets of miscellaneous reading ever printed."—*Saturday Post.*

" The Nights of the Round Table exhibit much fine, healthy feeling, forcible delineation of character, beauty of description and strength of thought, all clothed in elegant and nervous language."—*Aberdeen Herald.*

" Mrs. Johnstone's Tales may be generally characterized as carrying instruction with amusement. Many of them contain striking pictures of virtuous poverty, and of self-denial in the middle ranks of life, drawn in a piquant and pleasing style. We reckon it no small recommendation of these tales, that in them the common-place virtues of every-day life obtain more justice than in most novels of the day."—*Dundee Advertiser.*

No. IV.—SKETCHES OF IMPOSTURE, CREDULITY, AND FANATICISM. Price 25 Cents.

" This is a work of no common interest and research; it depicts the follies of the human mind in its various stages of ignorance ; a remarkable feature of an enlightened and scientific age is the disappearance of many, if not most of the monstrous beliefs and modes of deception under which our race has lived and been imposed upon. It is a work not merely for the gratification of the present moment, but one which will be read by successive generations with interest and instruction."—*Smith's Weekly Volume.*

" A most curious and interesting work."—*Protestant Churchman.*

No. V.—THE OPIUM WAR ; BEING RECOLLECTIONS OF SERVICE IN CHINA. By Captain Arthur Cunynghame. Price 25 Cents.

" Interspersed throughout are capital anecdotes, comic stories, and amusing personal adventures; but there is also a good deal of political information communicated carelessly, as if the writer was not anxious to show that he has thought much of the subject. All, therefore, who would peruse the most vivid and animating account of the splendid closing scenes of the Chinese war, must necessarily resort to Captain Cunynghame's volumes."—*Foreign Quarterly Review.*

" Captain Cunynghame's narrative of the British campaign in China, is a brief but most novel and entertaining glimpse of the celestials and the *fun* that Her Gracious Majesty's fleet and army had with the celestial boobies: the British brag about their war with the celestials, but we think there is not much glory in not being frightened with wooden artillery painted to the life, the noise of gongs, and celestial warriors dressed up in tiger skins, who, when they find they can't frighten the ' outside barbarians' in this way, take to their heels, and instead of fighting like *tigers,* run away like *rabbits!* What glory for Her Majesty's army and navy to encounter and conquer such an enemy !"—*Wayne Co. Herald.*

No. VI. — IMPRESSIONS OF IRELAND AND THE IRISH. By the author of " Random Recollections of the Lords and Commons," " The Great Metropolis," &c. Price 25 Cents.

" The most agreeably entertaining work that has for many a day met our view."—*Jackson (Tenn.) Republican.*

" An entertaining work."—*Jeffersonian.*

No. VII.—DONALDSON'S EVENTFUL LIFE OF A SOL-
DIER.   Price 25 Cents.

" One of the most pleasantly written and instructive books
of the kind ever published. The author served many years in
the peninsular campaigns, and although he seems to have escaped the worst effects of a soldier's life upon the character,
his narrative furnishes the strongest proofs of the evils of
war."—*Smith's Weekly Volume.*

No. VIII.—DUNN'S HISTORY OF THE OREGON TERRI-
TORY AND BRITISH NORTH AMERICAN FUR
TRADE.   Price 25 Cents.

" One of the latest and most informing books on the Oregon
Territory. The author naturally takes the British side of the
question, but according to the old maxim, *fas est ab hoste do-
ceri,* it cannot but be deeply interesting in the present posture
of affairs."—*U. S. Gazette.*

" The unconcealed hostility of Mr. Dunn injures the cause
he advocates, and will give offence in America, without
affording satisfaction here. The work, however, contains
much, and of interest, about which there need be no discus-
sion: a rapid sketch of the History of the Oregon Settlement,
of the Hudson's Bay and other fur-trading companies, an interesting account of the fur trade, and of those engaged in it,
with characteristic anecdotes and illustrations of the habits
and manners of the native Indians."—*London Athenæum.*

NO. IX.— NARRATIVE OF THE MUTINY AT SPIT-
HEAD AND THE NORE.   Price 25 Cents.

"One of the most interesting episodes in British history, and
comparatively little known."—*Smith's Weekly Volume.*

GREAT LITERARY ENTERPRISE.

BOOKS BY MAIL!

The "Waldie" System Revived by the Original Editor.

The cash system carried to its utmost limit by a reduction of one half.

TEN COPIES FOR $2 50 PER ANNUM EACH!!

On the first of January, 1845, was commenced at Philadelphia the publication of SMITH'S WEEKLY VOLUME, a Select Circulating Library for town and country, on the plan of Waldie's, at a greatly reduced price, of a larger size and new type.—Conducted by the original, and for the first seven years, the sole editor of Waldie's Library, and published by his son.

The plan embraces the publication of the newest and best

books in the various departments of Travels, Voyages, Tales, Sketches, Biography and Memoirs; in short, the whole range of polite literature, and including translations made expressly for the work.

TERMS.

" THE WEEKLY VOLUME, OR SELECT CIRCULATING LIBRARY," is printed on a double super-royal sheet, sixteen pages quarto, three columns on each, and mailed weekly with great care, so as to carry with perfect safety to the most distant post office.

*** JOURNAL OF BELLES LETTRES. By thus increasing the size of the paper, we occupy, without decreasing the quantity of book-matter, the two first pages as a Journal of Belles Lettres, formerly printed as a cover.

The whole will be printed and finished with the same care and accuracy as book work. The price is four dollars for fifty-two numbers of sixteen quarto pages each.

A club of three for ten dollars, or $3 33 each.

A club of five for fifteen dollars, or $3 each.

A club of ten for twenty-five dollars, or $2 50 each.

But in no case can the publication be forwarded, unless the order is accompanied with the remittance.

☞ Postage of this periodical, under thirty miles free; one hundred miles and under, one cent; over one hundred miles, one and a half cents.

A specimen number will be forwarded, without charge to all who request it, postage paid.

LLOYD P. SMITH, Publisher.

No. 19 St. James' Street, running from 6th to 7th, above Market, and directly in the rear of St. James's Church.

Philadelphia, 1845.

☞ A few complete sets of the back numbers are still on hand.

HOME & TRAVELLER'S LIBRARY,

A Serial of Popular and Standard Literature, in which the following Works are published:—

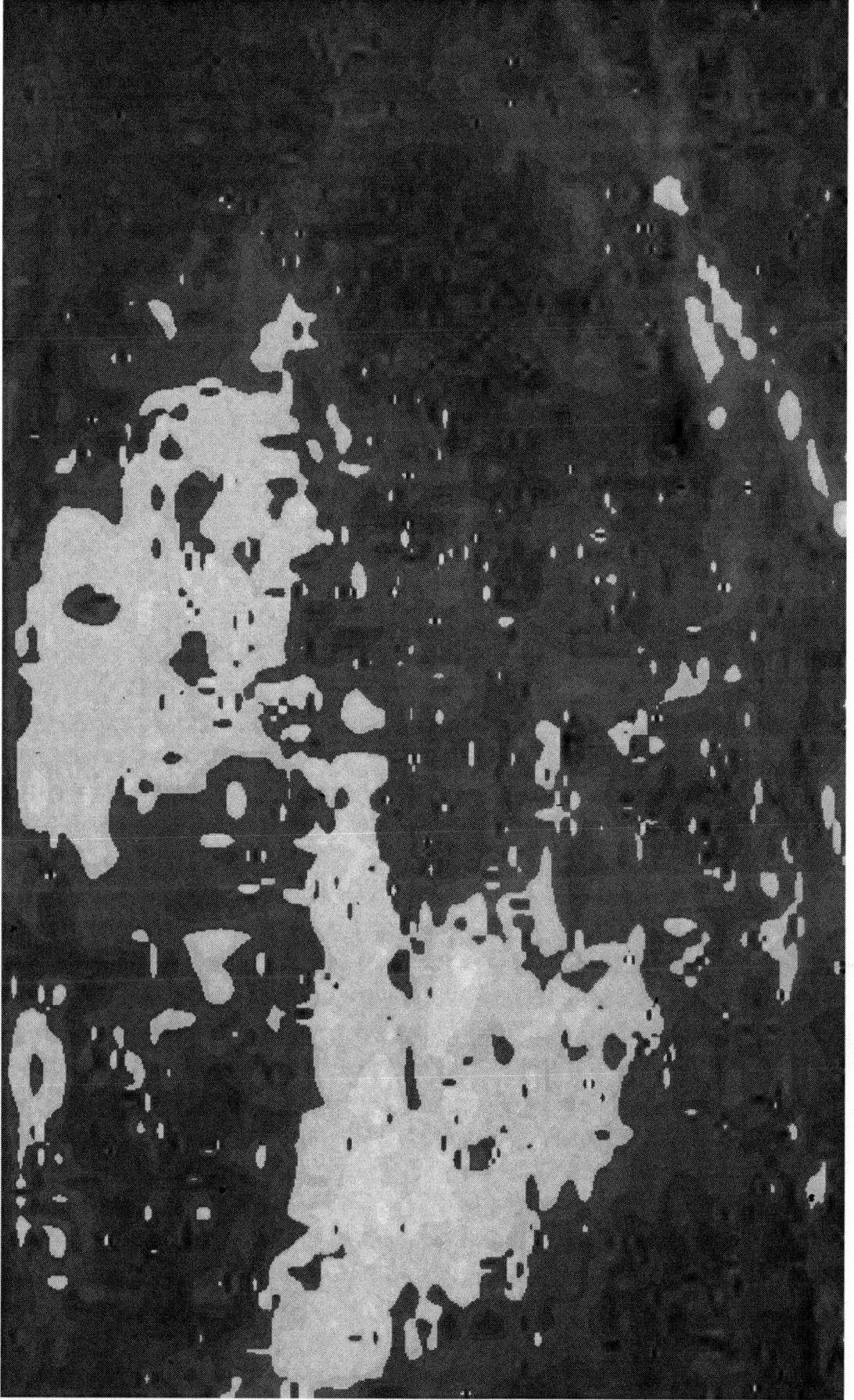

CPSIA information can be obtained at www.ICGtesting.com
Printed in the USA
LVOW051606130212

268486LV00013B/176/P

9 781149 511527